A Rhetoric For A Formation of Intention

Edward R. Heidt

A Rhetoric For A Formation of Intention

Edward R. Heidt

International Scholars Publications
San Francisco - London
1995

P
302.4
.H45
1995

Library of Congress Cataloging-in-Publication Data

Heidt,Edward R., 1946-

A rhetoric for a formation of intention / Edward R. Heidt.

    p. cm.--(Catholic Scholars Press)
    Includes bibliographical references and index.
    ISBN 1-883255-63-5: $64.95 - ISBN 1-883255-62-7 (pbk.): $44.95
    1.Discourse analysis. 2.Intentionality(Philosophy)
3.Biolinguistics. 4.Criticism. I.Title. II.Series: Catholic Scholars Press (Series)
P302.4.H45 1995
808 .0014--dc20   94-12137
                                    CIP

Editorial Inquiries:
International Scholars Publications
7831 Woodmont Avenue #345
Bethesda,MD.20814

To order: (800) 55-PUBLISH

Table of Contents

INTRODUCTION

What is the process by which a person forms intentions to participate in particular actions or speak or write certain words? How does the person articulate this process using the tools of language? Varieties of disciplines converge on these questions. Scientists and biologists examine and study the neurochemistry of the brain. Philosophers, moralists and psychologists attempt to define intentionality using the rhetoric of epistemology, phenomenology, science and philosophy. Rhetoricians and linguists carefully analyse the language and the literature of these disciplines and their varieties of forms of writing and speaking as a means to discover, uncover, intentions and intention–formation processes.

My argument in this book is that a significant part of the process of forming intentions involves the linguistic/rhetorical aspect of self–interpretation and self–translation. The multiple and diverse neurochemical forces at work in the human brain are organised and articulated through language; and literature mirrors these processes. In my analysis, I will be considering the intentional structure in terms of speech act theory's illocutionary forces and Derrida's metaphysics of presence; the behavioural structure in terms of observable, scientific evidence as bracketed by Husserl; and the verbal structure in terms of Chomsky's transformational grammar. And I will be considering the verbal structure in terms of how completely it represents or mediates the other two to each other.

The book is divided into five chapters, an introduction, and a conclusion. The first chapter situates the problem of the relationship among the three areas of intentional, verbal and behavioural. The three are in mutual, contextual configuration. They each have their own internal juxtaposition of perspectives. The intentional consists of the invisible, interior forces; the behavioural of the external, observable events and activities; and the verbal of the rhetorical, the words, of a particular language.

Chapter Two focuses specifically on the intentional structure as a neurochemical configuration in the brain of philosophical beliefs, desires, motivations, attitudes, feelings etc. The intentional structuring of these forces is the first, primary, central world from which words and behaviours proceed and where they are constituted. Words, behaviours and intentions become mirrors of each other with intentions and motivations being primary. The activity of the forces in consciousness and intention formation is an activity of equal weight and significance to the activity of speech and behaviour which proceeds therefrom. In other words, an activity of a murder with no apparent motive is a behavioural execution of some nexus of activity occurring within. When two individuals vow to love each other as husband and wife for the rest of their lives, the activity of the verbal structure, the words of the vow, is parallel to and of equal weight with the activity occurring within in the intentional structuring of forces.

The neurochemical configuration of philosophical beliefs is expressed in language. The machine/computer metaphor most closely approximates the workings of the brain and its structures which structured brain can be then examined as a phenomenological object which processes information and forms intentions. The language of the disciplines of philosophy and biology inform this chapter.

Chapter Three looks at the verbal and behavioural structures as visible representatives of the invisible intentional activity and process. In this chapter, the problems of reference, transition and transformation are raised. The internal, invisible, intentional activity needs to be transformed and translated into a language or a behaviour if it is to be known at all. The words and the behaviours transform the intentional structures of the individual speaking and/or behaving so that others can perceive and understand. Speech act theory's distinction between performative and constative issues in this chapter serve to illustrate how the intentional structure, as constative, can be successfully represented in and by the verbal and the behavioural, as performatives. Verbal and behavioural structures are constituted in the intentional. This verbal structure is mediatory and explanatory. Using Chomsky and others, I will show how language is a way to structure consciousness and intention effectively. I will show how language is basically a process of self-translation, where the interior forces are shaped and transformed into intentional systems in a computer-like language which is unique to the individual. The individual then uses the tools of a particular language structure to translate again for others who speak that language and live in that culture.

Chapter Four is a close reading of four short narratives which exemplify the theory detailed in the first three chapters. Thomas DeQuincey narrates the story of the day that he left Manchester at seventeen years of age and his narration discusses the significance of intention and the importance of intention formation in the writing. Geoffrey Chaucer narrates the love story of Troilus and Criseyde but does so with particular focus on the intentional structure of those two characters. And Graham Greene analyses the beginnings of an extramarital affair from the point of view of intention formation in his novel, *The End of the Affair*. Henry Fielding analyses another romantic relationship gone wrong in his "Unfortunate Gilt" chapter of *Joseph Andrews*. Many fiction writers represent this problem through interior monologues of their characters.

Chapter Five basically attempts to integrate Derridean deconstruction with an area that seems not to admit it or appears antithetical to it: religion. Biblical/dogmatic fundamentalism is shown to be "deconstructible" without losing its integrity.

Formation of intention can occur at three levels then:

1. In the natural biochemistry of the brain itself as a living organism. Psychologists and medical doctors have drawn attention to the fact that biochemical imbalance can affect judgement, intention and motivation.

2. In the behaviours of individuals. Behaviourists watch a person perform and deduce intentions and motivations therefrom.

3. In the words written or spoken by individuals. Linguists and rhetoricians note that intention formation and motivation can be articulated here.

However, I am arguing that in all three areas, language and rhetoric are essential to an understanding of the process. Philosophy, literature and rhetoric can inform the process which psychology and medicine also study.

In my conclusion, "The Affective and Intentional Fallacies Revisited," I focus closely on the Wimsatt and Beardsley texts and thesis that placing intention and affect about a text in the author is a false move. I argue that if I cannot say what a specific author's intention or motivation was in writing a particular text and if I can't say what the true emotional impact of the text is or should be, then I conclude that there are linguistic/rhetorical elements in the text itself which may support intentional–affective truths apart from reader and author. I use Samuel Beckett's *Happy Days* here and focus particularly on the enigmatic character, Willy.

CHAPTER ONE

The Relationship Among the Three Structures: Verbal, Behavioural, Intentional

only add
Deeds to thy knowledge answerable, add Faith,
Add Virtue, Patience, Temperance, add Love,
By name to come called Charity, the soul
Of all the rest: then wilt thou not be loath
To leave this Paradise, but shalt possess
A paradise within thee, happier far.

John Milton
Paradise Lost, Book XII, 581-587

At the outset, and by way of continuing the introduction, I wish to clarify and illustrate my understanding (that is, my presumptions and assumptions) about how individuals' intentional, verbal and behavioural structures are in an interrelational gestalt with each other whenever individuals undertake to form and/or explain and/or execute their intentions in and through words and behaviours.

The intentional structure, where particular intentions are formed as a prelude to the specific words or behaviours which incarnate them, or where particular intentions are re-examined in order to explain particular past words or actions, there exists a nexus of intentional forces. The verbal structure, where the intentions and behaviours are explained and/or defended, and which is a behaviour in its own right, consists of an arrangement of words, sentences, clauses and phrases in a particular language and arises from a particular culture. And finally, the behavioural structure, similarly, consists of an observable sequence of events or

6

activities (part of which are spoken or written words). Behaviours take place in the world of cause and effect, time and place, whereas the intentions are formed in an interior world where cause and effect, time and space are distorted. Language attempts to capture and mediate these interior and exterior worlds.

The major point that I develop in this book is that the interior, intentional structure is the primary world to be examined by the individual on the way to explaining or defending particular words or behaviours. Therefore, literacy, facility with one's native language, is an essential component in this communication of one's intentional structures. I believe that this thesis has significant impact not only on the importance of language acquisition and facility with one's language, but on larger social, political and moral issues as well.

I refer to the interior world of the intentional structure itself or the world of the verbal structure itself or the world of the behaviour itself as rotating around each other in a nexus of signification and exemplification depending upon which world I choose to focus on and structure. One of them may become more important than the other depending upon the particular case. When I proceed to structure one of these worlds, I discern nexi or clusters of relational elements (intentional forces, arrangements of words, sequences of actions) which comprise that world.

In other words, if I choose to focus on behaviours, I may look at the non-verbal social interactions of varieties of groups of people in varieties of countries and social contexts. If I wish to focus more clearly on moral issues, I will want to look carefully at intentional structures and how individuals form intentions to perform moral acts. But in any case, the language, the rhetoric, used to explain the non-verbal, social interactions or a moral stance is the key, mediating device, and so literacy, facility with language, is crucial.

For Plato, the real, the first, the primary world is that of unseen, absolute forms (universals) on which the secondary world, the world perceived by the senses, is based. Art, imitation or representation, is a third remove, a third world, away from this primary, first world of forms which first world can be observed in the second world of sense perception and appearance.[1] I wish to

---

[1] Plato, *The Collected Dialogues of Plato Including the Letters*. Edited by Edith Hamilton and Huntington Cairns. (Princeton University Press: Bollingen Series LXXI, 1961), Books III and X of the *Republic* generally outline these three worlds, but specific sections are III, 394c, e (p. 639), X, 598b, 600c (p. 823), and 611c (p. 836).

employ this Platonic structuring in my own taxonomy of a first, primary world of intentional structure, a second world of explanatory verbal structures and a third world of behavioural structures.

In terms of the Platonic theory, the intentional structure would be the real world, the first, primary world of forms residing in the forces there and any behaviours or words that issue from that world create another structure at either a first or second remove from the real world of intentional forces. Plato's first world of unseen absolutes and universals parallels what I am calling here the world of interior, intentional forces in individuals; his secondary world of appearances and sense perceptions parallels my world of executed words and behaviours, based upon formed intentions; and his world of artistic renderings, representations, and commentaries on the second world of sense perception and appearance which is at a third remove from the real, primary world of universals would parallel my verbal structures, rhetoric and language, which attempt to articulate intentional structures which explain and/or defend behavioural structures.

Ideally, I would like the intentional structure to be the first world from which words and behaviours logically follow and explanations or commentaries about these are at a third remove. But, intentional, verbal and behavioural worlds and structures intersect with each other such that one of them can become the Platonic real world of so-called "absolutes and universals" and the others are at first and second removes. In other words, a particularly controversial external behaviour like a murder with no apparent motive may be a third world, at a distinct third remove from the primary, intentional structure of the person who did the murdering. The verbal structure then becomes a second world mediator between the murderer and the motives. The verbal structure itself, which attempts to explain, could in other cases be the first, primary world, the real world and the intentional-behavioural structures could be equally displaced from it as second and third worlds. In other words, explanatory words, vocabulary and syntax, rhetoric, could be constructed for intentions and behaviours not yet performed just as they can be constructed for intentions formed and behaviours already executed. The verbal structure then becomes the primary one, imprinting itself on the intentional, which then becomes one remove, and then on the behavioural, a third remove, an attempt to mimic, imitate the verbal. Verbal structures become the primary ones in the case of the marriage commitment where the intentional (the desire to be married)—behavioural (actually being married) worlds take their direction from the verbal statement. Or blackmail and gossip where individuals' lives are formed by the words spoken about them. Their intentions and actions are based upon words spoken about them. The question here is: Is art imitating reality, or vice versa? What is illusion? What is real? Fact? Fiction?

In Edward Albee's controversial play *Who's Afraid of Virginia Woolf?*, an interrelation of verbal-intentional and behavioural structures occurs. The play itself is a verbal structure of Albee's creative imagination. In it, he creates characters who execute verbal structures. Nick explains and defends how he came to know and marry his wife and move to a new city. The verbal explanation follows the behaviour which presumes an intentional structuring and gestalt of motivating forces. For Nick, his intentional structure is central, primary and integrated with his behaviour and his explanatory words are at a third remove.

But when George, another character in the play, distorts Nick's story in a retelling, the verbal structure then becomes primary and Nick says "I will be (act, think, speak) what you say I am."[2] Nick will model his intentions and behaviours on George's verbal structure. The intentional-behavioural structures become secondary to the verbal. Reality imitates art. Fiction becomes fact.

> Nick: Was this after you killed them?
>
> George: Maybe.
>
> Martha: Yeah. And maybe not too.
>
> Nick: Jesus.
>
> George: Truth and illusion. Who knows the difference, eh, toots? Eh, houseboy? . . . So be it.
>
> Martha: Truth and illusion, George, you don't know the difference.
>
> George: No. But we must carry on as though we did.
>
> Martha: Amen.
>
> (pp. 201–202)

---

[2] Edward Albee, *Who's Afraid of Virginia Woolf?* (New York: Atheneum Press, 1975), 150.

If intentional structures are as central and as primary as I argue, then the verbal structures of particular languages, the need for literacy, are equally as primary and significant because through language skill, rhetoric, individuals' intentional structures can be accessed and behaviours can be explained, even predicted. Literacy, facility with one's language, allows individuals to experience and structure their interior forces into intentional systems and communicate these in verbal structures. The verbal structure is in this case one remove from the intentional. But it is a key, secondary remove which attempts to represent directly the intentional structure and forces. Rhetoric, correlative with literacy, allows people to structure effectively their words and behaviours so that they communicate the intentional structure. And the process works in reverse. Rhetoric, language facility, allows individuals to explain and defend the intentional structures constituting words and behaviours already performed. This is basically what happens in a courtroom with controversial words and behaviours—defense and explanation are given.

The relationships between words and behaviours, intentions, motives, explanations and defenses are linked (and again sometimes not linked at all) in often random and uncertain ways, and it is my object to give some taxonomic, systematic structure to this randomness and uncertainty.

Both John Henry Newman and Kenneth Burke address this key question of the random and uncertain way that many people elect to group particular intentional forces with particular words or behaviours in a gestalt such that particular words or behaviours are explained, defended and justified by particular motivations or intentions. In an appendix to his *Apologia Pro Vita Sua*, Newman uses the examples of telling a lie (verbal) and accidentally murdering someone (behavioural).[3] He writes that the lie is the external, "material" act, while the "formal," interior intention, the force behind the act, is really to protect one's own or someone else's reputation. With the accidental murder example, Newman writes that the person's formal, interior intention is to defend himself, but he must commit a "material," external, behavioural act of murder. The same kind of casuistry has been associated with what moralists have called the prin-

---

[3] John Henry Newman, *Apologia Pro Vita Sua*, edited by David DeLaura, (New York: W.W. Norton and Company, 1968), 261.

ciple of the double effect with regard to abortion or the just war theory. A doctor may intend to remove a cancerous growth from a woman's uterus and in the process, a fetus will also be removed. The observable, scientifically accessible fact is that a tumour has been removed as well as an embryo. The formal intention, the force behind the action, is to save the life of the woman by removing the cancer. This formal intention is not observable or scientifically provable. The intention is not to remove the fetus and so commit an abortion, just as the intention in a war is not to kill people for its own sake; but these acts of killing cannot be avoided, or so it is argued, if the cancer is to be removed or if world peace is to be achieved. Certain evils must attend these. Verbal, behavioural structures can be at odds with the intentional and they can be justified, defended and excused when "right," "good" intentions are paired with "questionable" words or behaviours.

Kenneth Burke contextualises this kind of casuistry that randomly matches various intentional forces with particular controversial behaviours or words in the behavioural structures in order to justify behaviours that are questionable or controversial. The primary force or motive to save the life of the woman is paired with a secondary, less important, act of abortion and a primary act of removing a tumour. In the case of a lie, the primary force or intention is to protect one's reputation and the actual speaking the words of the lie is secondary. Burke says that in these cases of protecting one's life or reputation or removing the cancerous growth, there is rather a nexus of forces, a "nexus of exemplification"[4] at the intentional level as there is a similar nexus at the behavioural and verbal. The verbal, rhetorical structuring can privilege particular intentional forces and behaviours over others.

Burke talks about Brentano's "nexus of exemplification" as a "perspective among perspectives,"[5] a hierarchy of perspectival elements (intentional forces, behaviours, words). Individuals freely situate attitudes, feelings, ideas, facts, intentions, intuitions, motives to which they have access into a hierarchy

---

[4] Aquila, Richard, *Intentionality: A Study of Mental Acts*, (The Pennsylvania University Press, 1977), 74.

[5] Kenneth Burke, "The Four Master Tropes," in *A Grammar of Motives*, (Los Angeles, The University of Southern California Press, 1969), 503.

of relations and values, a gestalt or nexus of exemplification, some of which are more important than others. Particular desires can be paired with particular beliefs as motivators of those beliefs. An amorphous, pre-verbal, subconscious intuitive force may motivate a particular desire which results in the formulation of a nexus of interior, intentional attitudes or convictions. This situating of particular motivations, feelings and desires in relation to particular beliefs, attitudes and convictions in one construct as opposed to another creates the intentional situation as well as the intentional problem. Another doctor (or the woman herself) may not be willing to remove the cancerous growth if it means removing the fetus. Other individuals may risk having their reputations ruined or being physically harmed if the alternative means telling a lie or harming someone else. The problem arises when a particular intentional structure, a gestalt of interrelated forces focusing on one issue (like abortion, lying, murder, or war) interacts with a completely other intentional structure, a gestalt of interrelated forces which focuses on a completely different issue (like saving a life or a reputation, defending oneself, world peace). The interrelational network becomes infinite as the range of objects, issues, and forces multiply.

Newman wrote an entire treatise on *The Grammar of Assent* in which he elaborated his key notion of "the ilative sense," which he describes as a kind of sixth sense, as part of the intentional structure of motivating forces:

> I have already said that the sole and final judgement on the validity of an inference in concrete matter is committed to the personal action of the ratiocinative faculty, the perfection or virtue of which I have called the Ilative sense, a use of the word "sense" parallel to our use of it in "good sense," "common sense," a "sense of beauty," etc;— . . . .[6]

In Newman's *Apologia* itself, his defense of his conversion from Anglicanism to Roman Catholicism ultimately is based upon this ilative sense or, as he says in the *Apologia*, on his right to private judgement (interior, intentional life) based upon his accumulation of logical sets of probabilities forming a

---

[6] John Henry Newman, *An Essay in Aid of a Grammar of Assent*, in *Victorian Literature: Prose*, edited by G.B. Tennyson and Donald J. Gray (New York: Macmillan Publishing Company, Inc., 1976), 433.

verbal argument, which argument approves and complements the private judgement, the ilative sense, to make a behavioural choice, a decision, with a reasonable degree of intellectual certitude and conviction but which may not be logically explained and defended to others. Newman experienced his own intentional forces as organising themselves by means of this ilative sense, a speech act performative, into an innate language that he could translate for himself but not for others.

Kent Bach and Robert Harnish argue for a "mutual contextual belief"[7] system which parallels what I am saying here about a nexus of exemplification and a gestalt of interrelated forces, words and behaviours. Their point is that individuals' particular unique systems, contextual interrelations, are made available to others through the mutuality of language. Their fundamental point is that a communicable structure can be created for the interior, intentional, attitudinal life.

For Bach and Harnish, to express an attitude, an intention, a desire is to intend that others take one's utterance as reason to think and believe that one has that attitude, intention or desire. For this intention to be fulfilled, the hearer must identify it on the basis of what is said together with other beliefs, desires, attitudes and intentions.

Mutual contextual belief systems distinguish norms, practices, rules, roles, subdivisions, collectivities, types, groups, and their structural organisations. They interlock and exhibit patterns which can be correlated with beliefs and attitudes shared by other systems in the individual's intentional structures and then these systems can network with other individuals' systems thus creating a "mutual context of belief." There may be a perceived consensus of opinion, an interpretation of perspectives, a reciprocity of perspectives; norms and conditions of accepted behaviour that people in particular societies and cultures follow in order to conform, be like others. There exist in all varieties and kinds of systems co-ordinative rules, cooperative rules, collective rules and regulations for driving, standing in line, activities that co-ordinate people effectively and guide their interaction; community actions like recycling, ecology, conservation of energy; the promulgation of rules by recognised authorities; all of which make

---

[7] Kent Bach and Robert Harnish, *Linguistic Communication and Speech Acts*, (Cambridge, Massacheusetts: The MIT Press, 1979), xv.

13

explicit the intersubjective, interrelational character of various social roles, characters, positions, types and expected behaviours. I am focusing here specifically on the intentional structure of an individual person, as a microcosm, a miniature of the larger intersubjective, interrelational structures of society. In other words, a convergence of Newman's ilative sense where a number of individuals have the same sense.

The Verbal Structure

I would like to review briefly the elements of the world of the verbal structures to demonstrate how they serve the intentional-behavioural. When words in any language are put together to form phrases, clauses and sentences and when sentences are arranged to form paragraphs, and paragraphs become essays and essays become chapters of books and books become instalments in series, there is a structuring of signification. There is a "transitivity of relations," as Jerry Fodor calls it.[8] A single word is meaningful only in its relation to another word at which time a relation of significance and transitivity of some kind is established. When a third word enters the group, new relations are again established. This is the basis for Derrida's principle of *differance* which argues that everything is defined by its relation to and difference from other things.

Words group together to form sentences, consisting of subjects, predicates, objects, clauses and phrases. Each of these elements takes on a relational role in the functioning of the sentence. Subjects, predicates and objects are primary; adjectives, adverbs and their clauses and phrases are secondary; conjunctions are tertiary. If I write about a larger unit like an essay or a book, then some entire sentences will function as primary expressions of major elements or secondary elements which describe the primary and tertiary elements (entire sentences which function like conjunctions) to make the book or essay cohere. What the words attempt to do is communicate the thought process of a particular individual. Just as particular thoughts, feelings, attitudes, intentions, interior

---

[8] Jerry A. Fodor, "Private Language, Public Languages," in *The Language of Thought*, (New York: Thomas Y. Cromwell Company, 1975), 89.

forces take on a relational aspect, so do the words and sentences if they are to communicate truthfully and effectively the interior structure.

A significant point here regarding a rhetoric for a formation of intention in a particular language is that sometimes the rhetoric can seriously distort the intention and meaning. I am arguing that literacy facility in language should actually build a rhetorical style which is effective and clear in its communication.

Noam Chomsky's revolutionary theory of transformational grammar elaborates this fact that the surface, verbal structure of various words and sentences is a way to access the innate, interior, intentional structure in consciousness[9] where the grammar is generated and transformed. Using the elements of the verbal structure and the awareness of the relation among elements in a sentence or a paragraph or an essay, individuals can access the varied structures of their intentional system of forces. Chomsky's point is that the words and verbal constructions are avenues to the structure of forces in the intentional structure. Similarly, the words in verbal structure are avenues to the detailed structure of the sequence of events in the external, observable event. There are elements in relation (actions, behaviours) that comprise a particular event, an activity, which elements can be communicated by using words, verbal structures. Objective, observable events can be transformed into verbal structures, which put the verbal structure at one remove from the event itself at the same time that it makes itself central, as word. The event is primary, central, real, until attention is diverted to the words which represent the event, and then they become primary and central and the two juggle for position.

Intentional, interior forces and structures can also be transformed into a verbal structure, which puts the intentional structure at one remove from the forces, which then are at a third remove from the words. Interior forces juggled into intentional systems and constructs about particular behaviours and expressed in language are three separate worlds juggling for position. The forces are central until which time they are organised and systematised and so the organisation and system become central. The verbal structure is mediatory, and

---

[9] Noam Chomsky, "The 'Innateness Hypothesis' and Explanatory Models of Linguistics," Chapter One of *Readings in Philosophy of Psychology*, Volume 2, edited by Ned Block, (Harvard University Press, 1981), 349.

therefore central, in the sense that it "propositionalises"[10] (organises, structures) random interior forces (neurochemistry) or the external behaviours.

The central problem is that these three worlds (the intentional, verbal and behavioural) cannot be simply and neatly categorised and separated into relations juggling for position. They have relations within each of them which are also juggling for position. There are separations, gaps, absences, transitions and interconnections which create Brentano's "nexus of exemplification" or Burke's "perspectives among perspectives" for a particular situation, and it is important that individuals determine which world (intentional, verbal, behavioural) they are focusing on as primary, and then focus on the relations in that world and then how the other two relate.

The Interior Structure

Because of the ever-changing neurochemical structure of the brain and possible imbalances there, the intentional structure of forces constantly changes. There are subconscious, preconscious, unconscious "traces"[11] which are either not accessible or are accessed by a neurochemical transmission at some later time, triggered[12] by some later input. An experience at two years of age, an experience unremembered but "traced" in consciousness, may be accessed in any number of later, remembered experiences. Therefore, as I proceed to discuss the elements in the three worlds of intentional, verbal and behavioural structures, it is important to recognise that new intersections, new possibilities, new explanations and formations are always occurring in the intentional structure where they

---

[10] Alonzo Church, "Propositions and Sentences," in *The Problem of Universals*, (Notre Dame: University of Notre Dame Press, 1956.) 276.

[11] Jacques Derrida, *Of Grammatology*, translated by Gayatri Chakravorty Spivak (Baltimore: The Johns Hopkins University Press, 1974), 61. Derrida uses Freud's Mystic Writing Pad much like Thomas DeQuincey's "palimpsest" image indicating that traces are always imprinted but also always erased or covered over by other traces.

[12] Fred Dretske, "Why Thinking Helps," unpublished manuscript, 19. In this article, Dretske uses the examples of "internal indicators" in frogs which trigger the response to catch a fly, in furnaces which trigger it to turn on and heat the room, in individuals which trigger that their finger go up or trigger that they intend to drive to Minnesota.

cannot occur in a past behavioural structure or verbal, explanatory structure. "Once a word is uttered [or a behaviour executed] it is irrevocable."[13] The point is that the static, stationary, verbal and behavioural structures, structures formed and constructed in a permanent way, may be a way, according to transformational grammar and speech act theory, to access the forces of the intentional structure and the threads and details (the complex of other persons, words, events) of the behavioural world.

The intentional structure of forces which constitutes the motivation for behaviour can be grouped into its own gestalt of forces as can the re-capitulation of the series of events in a controversial behaviour. They are in "modal"[14] relation within themselves and to each other. The intentional structure of forces, the controversial behaviour and the verbal, explanatory structure are in an "allomorphically sensitive context"[15] in which elements, forces, activities and words are in an "allomorphic," contextual[16] arrangement and rearrangement as a way to imitate the everchanging world of the intentional structure.

A primary element in the rhetorical structure of language is an element called a sentence which has words which relate to each other as subject and predicate and secondary elements like adjectives, adverbs and their clauses and phrases which expand and develop the subject and predicate by referring to them and/or describing them. "The universal plan underlying languages, with auxiliaries and inversion rules, nouns and verbs, subjects and objects, phrases and clauses, case and agreement, and so on, seems to suggest a commonality in the brains of speakers, . . ."[17] The primary elements in the sentence structure of the language, the subject and predicate, as a unit which expresses a complete

---

[13] Thomas DeQuincey, *Confessions of an English Opium Eater*, Volume 1 of *The Works of Thomas DeQuincey*, (London: The New Universal Library: George Routledge and Sons, Limited), 85.

[14] Roger Fowler, "The Referential Code and Narrative Authority," *Language and Style*, Volume 10, 1978, 139.

[15] Fred Dretske, "Referring to Events," *Midwest Studies in Philosophy*, II, 1977, 92.

[16] Isabel Hungerland, "Contextual Implication," *Inquiry*, 1960, 211.

[17] Steven Pinker, *The Language Instinct*, (New York: William Morrow and Company, Inc., 1994), 43.

thought, attitude, feeling or sentiment originating in and generated from the intentional structure of forces, may or may not be primary in the world of the intentional structure as it is in the verbal structure; nor may it be primary in the
world of a particular behaviour. The primary element in the verbal structure, the
sentence with a subject and predicate, may represent and communicate a part of
the external, controversial behaviour but it may express only that part of the behaviour which is secondary in the gestalt of events comprising the behaviour.

I want now to illustrate how the elements in the verbal structure (sentences, clauses and phrase, conjunctions) generated are a transformation of the
structure of intentional forces or the more integrated picture of the sequence of
events in the observable behaviour. The verbal structure thereby performs a
mediatory function, an apparently central, primary function, in that it expresses
the intentional structure constituting a behaviour or it is describing the cause and
effect sequence of a particular time-place behaviour.

In the *Theaetetus*, Plato makes the point that the soul is in continuous internal dialogue with itself:

> And do you accept my description of the process of think-
> ing? ... As a discourse that the mind carries on with itself ...
> when the mind is thinking, it is simply talking to itself, ask-
> ing questions and answering them, and saying yes and no.
> When it reaches a decision—which may come slowly or in a
> sudden rush—when doubt is over and the two voices affirm
> the same thing, then we call that its "judgement." So I
> describe thinking as discourse, and judgement as a statement
> pronounced, not aloud to someone else, but silently to
> oneself.[18]

[18] Plato, *Theaetetus*, in *Plato: The Collected Dialogues*, edited by Edith Hamilton and
Huntington Cairns (Princeton University Press, Bollinger Series LXXI, 1961), 895-6.

The Behavioural Structure

"I murdered them because they were there," confesses a murderer. The sentence itself is what I have been calling a verbal structure, a grammatical-rhetorical construct, which is a transformation of an intentional structure and is also an expression of what happened in the external-behavioural world. The central, primary world of the Platonic "real" is the external-behavioural, the scene of the murder itself. The verbal structuring of the events leading up to and surrounding the murder, and the verbal structuring of intentions and motivations of the murderer are removed from the real event itself; the verbal structuring is an attempt to re-present. The police and detectives focus on the behavioural world; lawyers, psychologists, moralists focus on the intentional world of the murderer. Police, detective, lawyer, psychologist and murderer alike use language to probe, communicate and analyse these two worlds of intention and behaviour.

The sentence, as a structure in itself, uttered by the murderer, has two primary elements consisting of subjects and predicates ("I murdered" and "they were there") and a tertiary element, a conjunction (because). Sentences need to be added to this sentence which would enlarge this description of the sequence of events in the behaviour and the motivations in the intentional structure. There would be more simple, compound, complex and compound-complex sentence arrangements. Clauses and phrases, adjectives and adverbs would be added as secondary, explanatory, descriptive elements. As the verbal structure elaborated itself, more and more access would be made available to the intentional structure of motivating forces in the murderer and external sequence of events in the behaviour.

In terms of the one available sentence itself, "I murdered them because they were there," a primary element in the external behaviour is explicated: that a murder occurred. The events leading up to and surrounding the murder could be put into language as relational elements which explain the sequence of events surrounding the murder. In terms of the intentional structure of forces in the murderer, the sentence is a primary element because it is confessional. It is an admission by the murderer that "murder" was apparently a primary force[19]

---

[19] John Searle and Daniel Vanderveken, *The Foundations of Illocutionary Logic*, (Cambridge University Press, 1985), 1. John Searle and Daniel Venderveken use this word "force" in explaining the thing that motivates the speaking of particular words, and I use it here as a word

within, which is surrounded by a gestalt of other forces that could also be verbalised.

This interior-intentional force which uses the word "murder" to represent itself also describes the activity in the external-behavioural structure and so it is both a noun and a verb in the verbal structure.[20] As a noun, it can be the subject or object in a sentence. As a verb, it can be the sentence's predicate; as a noun it can be both subject and object. That is, "Murder (subject) happens;" "I witnessed a murder (object);" "I murdered (verb)." In terms of the description of the external behaviour, it states the fact that the activity of murder occurred; a murder happened. The verbal structure has a referent outside of itself which referent is both an action (to murder—a verb) and an event (a murder—a noun) In terms of the description of the intentional structure of interior forces, it indicates, as a noun, that a state or gestalt of forces called "murder" exists there. As a verb, it indicates that there is an internal activity, a distinct force or impulse or series of forces or impulses, called "murder" circulating in some particular nexus of an individual's particular intentional structure. The word "murder" of course invites explication and explanation of both the behaviour and the intention. The word "murder" in the verbal structure invites the participation and inclusion of other words, constructed into sentences, which describe and explain the nexus of external activity surrounding the murder. As an activity and state in the murderer, it invites further explication and explanation of the nexus of forces surrounding it.

My point is that there is this nexus of forces within individuals which circulate around one another to form states, attitudes, dispositions which circulate around each other again. One particular nexus of forces (as an activity) forming a particular state (a noun) is not the only one and because of the nature of the neurochemical activity in the brain, they are always circulating and re-arranging. The explication of the events leading up to and surrounding a murder is an explication of a structure that is fixed in time and space. It is possible that the language could communicate a fairly full picture of all the details. But the verbal

---

to explain the motivations of behaviours as well.

[20] Jerry A. Fodor, "Private Language, Public Languages," in *The Language of Thought*, (New York: Thomas Y. Cromwell Company, 1975), 89.

structure cannot capture such a full, coherent portrait of the internal structure of intentional forces because they are in this constantly changing circularity; they cannot be fixed in space and time like external, observable behaviours can and like verbal structures themselves can. The interior forces which group to form intentional states and systems are always in intersecting motion and therefore, according to Derrida, "unreachable, untranslatable, inaccessible."[21] Courts sometimes acquit because of "temporary insanity."

The internal gestalt of intentional forces and systems circulating around a primary force like "murder" as expressed by the word "murder" is what I am calling a rhetoric for an examination of a formation of intention. A portrait of forces needs to be established which is in contextual integration with various external events and behaviours, which also need to be established in portraits of contextual integration. The relationship of the individual person to this formation, explanation or execution of each of these is central and crucial to the intentional structure, the verbal explanatory structure and the behavioural execution because only the individual can articulate the interrelations in each of the structures.[22]

I have outlined briefly here, in this first chapter, what I will elaborate more fully in subsequent chapters. An individual person's intentional structure can be systematised, arranged and rearranged in varying gestalts of ever-changing forces and groups or systems of forces. Specific behaviours of individual persons can also be structured into systems, arrangements of activities, events, in a sequence of cause and effect, located in time and space, which are fixed there and then fixed in the verbal representation. The verbal structure representing the behaviour is "fixed" until some new activity or event is discovered, some new detail is learned, which enlarges the sequence surrounding the whole activity. In this sense, the external behaviour is never fixed, like the internal, because new facts may always be discovered and added, comparable to the continuing neurochemical interactions.

If a behaviour has not occurred yet, but is contemplated and if the behaviour is controversial, then an examination of the intentional structure is mandated. If a

---

[21] Jacques Derrida, *The Ear of the Other: Otobiography, Transference, Translation*, translated by Peggy Kamuf, edited by Christie McDonald (New York: Schocken Books, 1985), 114-115.

[22] Robert C. Stalnaker, *Inquiry*, (Cambridge, Mass.: MIT Press, 1984), 15.

controversial behaviour like murder has occurred, then an examination of the intentional structure is also demanded but it may offer little or no explanation for the murder. Consequently, the behavioural structure of events surrounding the murder becomes central.

The verbal structure of individual language systems, I have been suggesting, is the mediating world, the way to access the structure of the intentional forces and a way to organise the external world of past controversial behaviours. The verbal structure can assist in the formation of intention; it can assist in the explanation of intention after a behaviour has been executed and it can be the basis from which a behaviour is executed. The presence and recognition of the forces in relation in the formation as well as the examination of an intention and the presence and recognition of the sequence of behaviours in a particular event in the explanation or execution of a behaviour can be accessed in and through the tools of the language. In terms of the Platonic triad of real world, physical world and artistic world, in the example of a murder with no apparent motive, the external-behavioural order and structure is the real, central, primary area of investigation and elaboration and the verbal structuring of this event is at one remove from it and the murderer's intentional structure, system of forces, is at a third remove. But in the example of the intention to murder at some future date, the intentional structure of forces is the real, central, primary world to be examined and investigated and the verbal structuring of this intentional system is at one remove from it and the actual execution of the murder is at a third remove. In the example of the intention to marry at some future date, although this is not a controversial event like a murder is, it involves an examination of the intentional structure of forces as the primary, central, real world to be examined and "formed" and translated into a verbal structure which is at one remove from it and then translated to the actual marriage itself which is at a third remove from it but whose execution is constituted by it.

The world of language, the verbal structures, the rhetoric, is the world which explains and describes both the intentional structure and the behavioural one. The verbal structure's capacity to explain and describe intention, motivation and behaviour also has the capability of connecting the intentional with the behavioural such that the one explains or complements the other in various ways. In this regard, I am considering the world of the verbal structure, the language, the rhetoric used, as the central, primary one, the Platonic "real" world of universals, absolutes, the world of "forms" upon which intention and behaviour are constituted. Individuals take the random forces within and structure them through, with and in language. The language, the verbal structure, then returns to the ever-changing, ever-developing random array of forces and converses with them and re-structures them, through language. "I murdered them because they were there" returns to the murderer and invites more language, more conversation, more structuring. "I will love only you for the rest of my life" returns to the speaker at various times and invites continued conversation and re-structuring. Language structures mediate the internal-intentional forces with words spoken and behaviours executed.

The verbal structures of languages are ways to explain, explore and form the random forces of the intentional life and structure it. Language and rhetoric also explain, explore and organise the possibilities for execution of intention in behaviour, and can re-organise and re-explain behaviours already performed, based upon new information, new input. In this sense, language, verbal structures and behaviours already performed are in effect frozen; they have occurred in time and space and nothing can change them, except re-editing, re-writing. But the interior life of intention formation is active and on-going; it is always re-editing and re-writing itself; it can never really be structured into a verbal icon; the verbal structure may capture only a part of someone's intentional life at a particular time and place, and even then, it captures only a part of the palimpsest of intersections.

The verbal structure's capacity to capture this interior life receives due attention from such philosophers and linguists as Jacques Derrida, Noam Chomsky, Edmund Husserl and John Searle. Jacques Derrida focuses on the ongoing activity in the intentional structuring in consciousness, whereas Husserl focuses on consciousness' attempt to form the phenomenological bracket, the structure of external experience, through which it captures the experience. Noam Chomsky shows how the verbal structure, the surface structure of the grammar, the rhetoric, the sentence structure is a way to access the structure of the intentional life. And John Searle writes about the structure of illocutionary forces as those which motivate speech acts. Individuals have ongoing "generations" of forces, which, when they attempt to articulate them in a language accessible to others, find that they must first transform them into a language, a rhetoric, accessible to themselves. Individuals perform a generative process of self-translation of these forces on the way to transforming them into the grammatical, syntactical, rhetorical structures of a particular language with which to communicate these to others.

There is then, first a self-translation of these random, Derridean forces and then a Chomskean re-translation of those into a particular language structure; each translation is based upon the individual's Husserlean bracketing of personal experience. In this sense, the Chomskean language structure is a secondary world to the real world, the primary world, of the Derridean intentional forces. Similarly, the verbal structure can also refer "out" to behaviours performed and witnessed by others as well as refer "in" to the interior life of intentions and intentional forces. The words and behaviours return to the individual as more raw materials which are incorporated by the individual.

For example, in the case of "I murdered them because they were there," there is a verbal structure, a sentence made up of 7 words, words which make sense together only in terms of their *differance*—their compilation as a compound sentence—two sentences joined by a conjunction. This verbal structure accesses, chronicles, organises, brackets an external fact, a behaviour. The behaviour occurred and the murderer (or the policeman, lawyer, whomever) uses language to communicate what happened. The sentence attempts to access the interior life of the murderer, the intentional forces which motivated him with "because they were there." Other sentences need to be constructed to fill out the details of the murder itself and the intentional forces which motivated it. The worlds of verbal structure, intentional structure and behavioural structure interrelate as primary, secondary or tertiary depending upon the perspective. The world of the murder as a behaviour is primary and central as an objective reality occurring in the world and affecting many people. The world of the verbal structure becomes central when it attempts to explain and articulate exactly what happened and why. But if the real world, the primary world, is that of the behaviour itself, then the verbal structure could be considered "one remove from it" and the intentional life and forces of the murderer at a third remove.

On the other hand, the real world is the interior life of intentional forces which constitute and form behaviour and is at a third remove from the real, primary activity of the life of the individual. The verbal structure, the rhetoric, grammar and syntax become primary, central and real to the extent that they mirror and bridge the two other worlds. The verbal structure becomes the real world when it dictates to the intentional and the behavioural and shapes them. When what I say or write returns to me and dictates how I feel, think and behave, then the verbal world is the central, the primary, the real one. Ideally, the verbal structure, the world of language, is meant to serve the intentional, to help it organise itself and its behaviours.

> *I'll have grounds*
> *More relative than this—The play's the thing*
> *Wherein I'll catch the conscience of the King.*

> William Shakespeare
> *The Tragedy of Hamlet, Prince of Denmark*
> Act II, scene ii, ll. 603-5

CHAPTER TWO

The Interior-Intentional Structure

"All you need say is "Yes" if you mean yes, and "No" if you mean no; anything more than this comes from the Evil One."

Matthew 5: 37

In this second chapter, I would like to focus systematically on the interior world of intention formation and the intentional structures in consciousness, thereby making them primary, and in so doing I will locate a nexus of forces or elements in those structures which will serve to assist in an understanding of how an intentions are formed.

I will execute this focus in the following ways in this chapter:

First, I would like to consider philosophically the straight-forward, physical, neurochemical workings of the brain as a preface to any structuring.

Secondly, I will discuss the intentional structure as one structure among many intentional systems of beliefs, desires, and motivations.

Thirdly, I will employ the metaphor of the machine, the computer specifically, in my consideration of the structuring of intentions.

And finally, I will consider the intentional structure as an object to be mapped, a phenomenological object to be constructed and studied.

A Philosophical Look
at the Physical, Neurochemical Workings

Jacques Derrida, in his writing, suggests that consciousness is a series of random, conscious, unconscious, subconscious and preconscious "traces."[1] Derrida gets his idea of these many traces in the mind from Freud's mystic writing pad through which Freud asserts that the mind is constructed not only of conscious but of unconscious, subconscious and preconscious conglomerates of traces; each trace having been "ploughed"[2] there at a different time and some have been ploughed over or 'written' over so often by the continuous onslaught of sense experience that they are inaccessible, however still there. Freud determines through this writing pad model that unremembered experiences of early childhood are still recorded on the mind but are recorded on that part of the mind called the unconscious, and these can be accessed when a later conscious experience causes an intersecting with these earlier subconscious or unconscious experiences, although the point of intersection and access may be quite confusing to the individual and may occur at unusual times.

By this concept of the trace or "tracing" on consciousness, Derrida means to suggest that a point of origin can never be discovered except reciprocally at parallel points of non–origin. In other words, a path of discourse in consciousness is a series of intersecting traces. There is no one trace at which point of origin is constituted.[3]

Derrida's comments suggest that this network of traces is a "metaphysics of presence."[4] Individuals are present to their intentional structures and they interact with these structures based upon this interior network of forces and traces. Persons are present to the outside world, in what I am calling observable, behavioural structures, in that "privileged position" of the "absolute now, the life in the present, the living present . . . ."[5] The essence of Derrida's metaphysics

---

[1] Jacques Derrida, *Writing and Difference*, (The University of Chicago Press, 1978), 223.

[2] Jacques Derrida, *Of Grammatology*, trans., Gayatri Chakravorty Spivak, (Baltimore: Johns Hopkins University Press, 1974), 287.

[3] Derrida, *Of Grammatology*, 61.

[4] Derrida, *Of Grammatology*, 74.

[5] Derrida, *Of Grammatology*, 309, 311.

hat the brain plays on individuals. New learning would correspond to
tion of new synapses or the activation of old, dead ones. Sagan argues
are then possible brain states that have never been occupied and an
; number of configurations that have never been entered or glimpsed.[12]
Iohandas Ghandi makes the same point introducing his autobiography:
e some things which are known only to oneself and one's Maker. These
rly incommunicable.[13] But, Ghandi says,

> one thing took deep root in me—the conviction that morality
> is the basis of things, and that truth is the substance of all
> morality. Truth (and later health), religion and the politics of
> non-resistance became my sole objective.[14]

And he always takes great care to listen to his own "inner voice," and
'religious spirit within [soon] became a living force."[15] And from his study
practice of law, he says that he was able "to find out the better side of
nan nature and to enter men's hearts."[16] His decisions and vows regarding
ting and vegetarianism and his vow of chastity are unified in the name of self-
ntrol; he believes that "the mind is at the root of all sensuality."[17] A person
ay "keep his body from food or sex but feast his mind upon all sorts of
.elicacies . . . . So long as thought is not under complete control of the will,
words and deeds are not."[18]

In this interior, neurochemical activity of becoming, philosopher Derrida
and autobiographer Ghandi suggest that individual persons, as beings, as persons who form intentions and attitudes, be allowed to construct and deconstruct

---

[12] Sagan, *The Dragons of Eden*, 30.

[13] Mohandas K. Ghandi, *Autobiography: The Story of My Experiments with Truth*, translated by
Mahadev Desai, (New York: Dover Publications, Inc., 1983), viii.

[14] Ghandi, 30. See p. 44 for further discussion of "truth in religion" and p. 78 for further
discussion of the politics if non–resistance.

[15] Ghandi, 115.

[16] Ghandi, 117.

[17] Ghandi, 183.

[18] Ghandi, 183-184.

of presence is in his ontological assertion that
"identified logocentrism [the word (λογοσ), articu
and writing] and the metaphysics of presence as t
tematic and irrepressible desire"[7] for signification
word and deed. He privileges the verbal structure ove.
munication of intention, although both word and deed o.
infinity of interconnected traces.

surprises
the gener
that ther
enormo'

There
are cl

Derrida's "natural attitude"[8] of the being, the indiv.
present is one that respects this on-going, intersecting act
the being, discussed by scientists and doctors in terms of n
missions and electrical impulses in the brain.[9]

Scientists have argued that "half or more of the brain
The Dragons of Eden, Carl Sagan points out that "some sort.
haviour are not very apparent from the outside, or even from the
are human perceptions and activities which may occur only ra
creativity." Sagan says that the human brain contains about "ten bil.
ing elements called neurons (which have between 1,000 and 10,000 s
links with adjacent neurons) which have electrical currents generate
and by them—electrical impulses transmitted along nerve fibers do,
neurochemical intermediaries initiate movements."[11]

th
a
t

Besides these neurons, scientific investigation has also determine
there are microcircuits capable of much wider range of more subtle and
responses. The human brain is characterised by 10 to the 13th power synap.
and thus the number of different states is unimaginably large. Because of th.
immense number of functionally different configurations, no two humans can
ever be really very much alike, which also accounts for the unpredictable

[6] Jacques Derrida, *Writing and Difference*, 207, 213, 277.

[7] Derrida, *Of Grammatology*, 49.

[8] Derrida, *Writing and Difference*, 144.

[9] Richard M. Restak, *The Mind*, (New York: Bantam Books, 1988), 40, 258-259.

[10] Carl Sagan, *The Dragons of Eden: Speculations on the Evolution of Human Intelligence*, (New York: Random House, 1977), 30.

[11] Sagan, 40-41.

themselves freely. "Natural writing in keeping with the natural attitude is that which is in communion with the unity of breath and voice; the pneumatological and the grammatological."[19] Derrida insists that persons

> must recover the *natural*—that is, the simple and original —
> ...*natural* bond of sense to the sense and it is this that passes from sense to sound: "the natural bond," Saussure says, "the only true bond, the bond of sound." The natural bond of the signified (concept of sense) to the phonic signifier would condition the natural relationship subordinating writing (visible image) to speech.[20]

Derrida speaks about these constructions of intention as violent "ruptures" of these "natural attachments"[21] which make traces in consciousness. Experiences are "enregistered" on consciousness as "breaches" or paths on that consciousness. He writes about this process as an "engraving, a groove, a relief, to a surface whose essential characteristic is infinitely transmissible."[22] Freud forges the hypothesis of "contact-barriers" and "breaching" (*Bahnung*, lit. pathbreaking) as the breaking open a path (a trace) (*Bahn*). "... Breaching, the tracing of a trail opens up a conducting path ... breaching without difference, resistance, is insufficient for memory."[23] This "breaking a path against resistance, rupture, and irruption becoming a route, is a violent inscription of a form."[24]

The physical, neurochemical activity in the brain and mind are infinitely more complex than we can imagine and have infinite potentiality for new reaches. These potentialities can be bracketed and expressed, limited, or they can be allowed to flourish and range in a continual process of becoming through the continual process of new input. "Being," in the sense of existing, is presence to one's own ongoing neurological activity and process of becoming.

---

[19] Derrida, *Of Grammatology*, 17.

[20] Derrida, *Of Grammatology*, 17.

[21] Derrida, *Of Grammatology*, 46.

[22] Derrida, *Writing and Difference*, 12.

[23] Derrida, *Writing and Difference*, 200-201.

[24] Derrida, *Writing and Difference*, 214.

When the neurological activity of the brain stops, the person either dies or lies in a hospital comatose, diagnosed as "brain-dead" to the extent that there is no electrical activity as registered on the encephalogram. A violence has happened to the brain. Similarly, if neurochemical activity increases, electrical activity is registered as increased, and this is yet another kind of violence. When an individual intentionally stops or starts examining some aspect of intentional structure and forms or explains that structure in some way, based upon examination, a violence is being done not only to the on-going process of becoming in that mind but also to the act of explanation itself. Neurological, neurochemical activity increases and can be registered on an encephalogram. Derrida feels that such increase and decrease in electrical activity and energy is a "violence" to the brain, causing it to change, reform. The construction of the speech, the written text, or the preparation to perform a behaviour, according to a philosopher like Husserl, is a natural way of expressing, bracketing, the activity in the mind.

Derrida sees such verbal or behavioural construction as a violence, a rupture, which reverses upon itself, convolutes so to speak, is "warped" or elliptical, as relativity theory says, and returns to the person from which it came and becomes an "other," a new input, and makes another trace, another mark, another path on the palimpsest of the brain and so allows for altogether new mental interactions.

In other words, individuals read what they wrote or watch themselves act or hear themselves speak and say "that is not me" or "that is not what I meant or intended." The verbal, behavioural structures return to them as something "other" which trace themselves on the consciousness and become other pieces of perceptual/conceptual input which can be used in a next construction of another word or behaviour at another time and place. The construct is deconstructed based upon the new configuration of mental perceptions, neurochemical firings in the brain.

> What else than a natural and mighty palimpsest is the human
> brain? . . . Everlasting layers of ideas, images, feelings,
> have fallen upon your brain softly as light. Each succession
> has seemed to bury all them before. And yet, in reality, not
> one has been extinguished . . . Yes, reader, countless are the
> mysterious handwritings of grief and joy which have in-

scribed themselves successively upon the palimpsest of your brain; . . . They are not dead but sleeping.[25]

A "palimpsest" is a document unearthed in the Middle Ages which contains the imprints of a series of writings accumulated on the surface of the document. Writing is erased from the document and other writings are placed over it, throughout its history. Archaeologists and paleontologists scrape and/or wash these surfaces in their search for traces of information about previous epochs and cultures and these documents with many layers of writing are called palimpsests.[26]

Thus, Derrida's key point is that everything on the palimpsest of the brain is always "under erasure."[27] There is "always already"[28] (his constantly recurring thematic phrase) present an "untouchable, untranslatable, absolute nonpresence"[29] that is buried (he says "erased") under the palimpsest of intersections and interactions (of words and behaviours).

> Rousseau . . . articulates the chain of significations ["a system of roots"] . . . on the classical metaphysics of the entity as *energy*, encompassing the relationships between being and time in terms of the now as being in action (*energeia*):[30]

> *Energeia* of speech (a word's capacity to make the image of the thing present in the mind back to the mind)[31] is a process of always supplementing and compensating for what is lacking in the previous articulation.[32]

[25] Thomas DeQuincey, *Tales and Prose Phantasies*, Volume XIII, *The Collected Writings of Thomas DeQuincey*, ed. David Masson (Edinburgh: Adam and Charles Black, 1890), 346.

[26] William Flint Thrall, Addison Hibbard and C. Hugh Holman, *A Handbook to Literature*, (New York: The Odyssey Press, 1936), 336-7.

[27] Derrida, *Of Grammatology*, 60, xxxix.

[28] Derrida, *Writing and Difference*, 74, 165, 178, 211, 213, 219, 226. *Of Grammatology*, 7, 9, 47, 49, 66, 73, 84, 106, 112, 280, 289-290, 304.

[29] Jacques Derrida, *The Ear of the Other*, 114-115.

[30] Derrida, *Of Grammatology*, 102, 311.

[31] Derrida, *The Ear of the Other*, 137.

[32] Derrida, *Writing and Difference*, 212.

32

> . . . this sequence of supplements . . . is an infinite chain,
> ineluctably multiplying the supplementary mediations that
> produce the sense of the very thing they defer: the mirage of
> the thing itself, of immediate presence, of imaginary percep-
> tion.[33]

> This movement of supplementary representation approaches
> the origin as it distances itself from it.[34]

This origin, this center which Derrida speaks about as a core, is ab-
solutely untouchable, the "asemic" kernel, the center beneath the shell of the
text.[35] The word "force," unlike the word consciousness, allows that there are
pre-verbal, preconscious, unconscious, subconscious activities, as in the sense of
an illocutionary *energeia*, going on in these untranslatable, inaccessible forces at
unreachable "centers" or origins of an individual where grammar, language and
intention formation generate and proceed to a level of mental representation, interior articulation, and construction of sentences which are different again from
the spoken or written text or the behaviour performed. This highly individual,
primitive, illocutionary activity is a "hermeneutical," heuristic activity which establishes itself as a network of "forces" among forces (an *energeia*) attempting
to give voice to the kernel, the core, Derrida's unreachable center, origin or
force.[36] The individual attempts to "seek a place that is always missing"[37] yet
always present because at the moment that individuals believe that they have
captured and constructed their intentional relations or some aspect of these relations in a word or act, the word or act returns to the person and engraves itself
as a new piece of input on the mind, changing the conception and perception of
the self, the mind, consciousness, intentions, attitudes, beliefs and desires, in an

---

[33] Derrida, *Writing and Difference*, 147.

[34] Derrida, *Of Grammatology*, 295.

[35] Derrida, *The Ear of the Other*, 80, 113.

[36] Derrida, *The Ear of the Other*, 136.

[37] Derrida, *Writing and Difference*, 178.

ongoing, Nietzschean "eternal return."[38] Individuals continually read and interpret themselves to themselves and others.

Derrida represents the activity of a mind, the formation of an intentional structure, as a continual, always already, free interplay of traces which imprint themselves on the mind, and this activity is violent because the engraving and the subsequent construction or bracketing, changes both the nature of the activity of the process of becoming and the creation of the text expressing that activity. Once an individual attempts to "compute" the syntactic structure of the activity of forming intentions, a violence occurs.

Simply, the sequence is as follows: there is in the mind a configuration of primitive, pre-verbal illocutionary forces and activities continually occurring and continually re-centering and re-focusing, re-configuring themselves. The configuring process is influenced by the continuous input of new overlaps, new experiences which cause a re-aligning, re-adjusting of the forces into a new juxtaposition, a new system of events, forces, references and descriptions.

The individual seeks to articulate the ongoing activity of these illocutionary forces at various unreachable centers, but the moment that such formation with a view to articulation, verbalisation, begins is not only a languaging moment of what I am calling a "rhetoric of intention formation," it is also moment of deconstruction, de-formation, or, more positively re-formation. Individuals intend to tell someone else in word or deed about this interior activity. The activity erupts in a word or behaviour and the person returns to examine the activity in an attempt to explain why the forces configured and erupted as they did.

Desires, Beliefs, and Motivations

Desires, and by extension motivations, like the words that express them, can be defined in terms of perceptions or other mental states; desires represent particular kinds of needs of the person; other names are given to other mental states to represent other needs, goals, attitudes, beliefs which will be thrust out-

---

[38] Friedrich Wilhelm Nietzsche, *Ecce Homo* and *The Birth of a Nation*, (New York: The Modern Library, Inc., 1927), 69, 95, 107.

34

side of the person's consciousness in word (speech or writing), behaviour, but the range of possible combinations of beliefs and desires forming mental, intentional states is infinite.[39]

Beliefs and desires and their various combinations and interrelations are dispositional, attitudinal states. They interconnect in any number of ways to form states which produce action. The action, the behaviour, may trigger a desire to look into the states, structures and formations from which the action came, and hopefully be able to predict future behaviours based upon such examination.

H.P. Grice in "Meaning Revisited" writes that an individual's beliefs and desires need to correspond to the real world of internal experience in order to be fulfilled and in order for the psychological mechanism to operate in a beneficial way. Grice creates a triangle of reality consisting of thought (intentional structure), language, and communication devices (verbal structure). Grice insists that individuals must co-operate (hence his "co-operative principle") in communicating their intentional structures to each other by being careful to follow certain rules like supplying enough quality information and following the rules of the grammar of their language. Grice insists that the word be a sign, an external marker, a signifier, that expresses, represents an interior, intentional reality. There is a finite system of syntactical operations and combinations, arrangements of signs, to express an infinite mental network. For Grice, individuals' rational-relational, interior-intentional systems of beliefs and desires are singularly important relations and systems to be communicated, and individuals are to use language to its best advantage to do so.

Robert Stalnaker calls belief and desire states "correlative dispositional states of a potentially rational agent."[40] Belief and desire are problematic not so much because they are not directly observable but because they are intentional; they are real causal properties of and for a person; they have a content, an internal structure of causal connections and individuals can use language to serve their beliefs and desires because effective use of language will communicate the

---

[39] Robert Stalnaker, *Inquiry*, (Cambridge, Mass.: MIT Press, 1984), 127.

[40] Stalnaker, 15.

beliefs and desires effectively, holistically, in a clear, integrated way rather than in an "atomistic,"[41] fragmented, disjunctive way.

Stalnaker's point is that there is a content to mental states. There are beliefs, desires, attitudes, feelings, which can be arranged and called by these names and collectively called "a content" and objectified in language. The pragmatic (functional/rational) aspect looks for logical explanations of behaviour as a representation of the consciousness constituting the behaviour while the linguistic aspect looks at the words used to express the state as representations of consciousness and depends upon linguistic, rhetorical sophistication and conceptual development. I shall look at this linguistic, rhetorical aspect more closely in Chapter Three.

The point I want to make here is that mental states consist of varieties of combinations of beliefs and desires and can be given sentential, rhetorical structure as the result of a computational synthesis that individuals perform on them and for themselves. The sentences and computations are materialistic, functional accounts of non-material realities. A belief relation is a composite relation of other states, and also involves a relation to the person's behaviours and language. Here I describe the belief-desire relation as separate from observable behaviours and utterances, but I do so as a prelude to the fact that observable relations and utterances are reciprocally constituted in the belief and desire relations of the intentional structures.

An interior, intentional state of an organism, like a brain, possessed by an individual, as in a state of believing or desiring something, is causally connected to inputs and outputs of other psychological states.[42] The question is: what are the laws by which the particular organism, the individual person's brain, is governed (apart from and in addition to neurochemical); and how does the intentional structure correlate with the behavioural and verbal; and how does it interact with the intentional-behavioural-verbal structures of other individuals in the world?

---

[41] Stalnaker, 16.

[42] Hartry Field, "Mental Representation," in *Readings in Philosophy and Psychology*, Volume Two, edited by Ned Block, (Harvard University Press, 1981), 89.

Stephen Schiffer summarises Stalnaker's treatment of these mentalistic relations (centers of rationality) (belief, desire relations) and semantic relations (meaning created, action motivated, propositions themselves located) in a huge causal nexus. Stalnaker sees this nexus of intentional relations as the "structure of inquiry;" an enterprise of forming, testing and revising beliefs, desires, intentions etc. In the first part of his book, he defines the nature of intentional mental states in terms of this nexus of natural relations of natural objects and systems within the person's consciousness. The problem, of course, is then representing this activity in words and behaviours which is a separate act in itself. He sees the problem of intentionality as a problem about the nature of representation, a language act.

> "How to give a piece of your mind; or, the logic of belief and assent" in which de Sousa argues that we should distinguish sharply between what he calls *belief* and *assent*. Belief, on his view, is a sort of lower, less intellectual phenomenon; it forms the dispositional foundation for the fancier phenomenon, assent, which is restricted to human beings.[43]

After quoting DeSousa, Donald Dennett proceeds to distinguish between beliefs, opinions, desires, and assents. "Notional" desire is the idea that the person might tend toward a particular direction while "relational" desire is that the person definitely needs and will tend in a particular direction.[44] Beliefs and opinions are those which inform desire and assent states. An individual can have an opinion about something which is not a belief; the opinion may not motivate desires but opinions may accumulate to form a belief, resulting in the assent of the will and some subsequent, external action or word, like Newman's conversion to Catholicism based upon his theory of accumulated probabilities indicating that belief and assent are a logical avenue to follow.

Dennett naturally, quite logically and clearly, makes "having a belief" stronger than "having an opinion," but opinions influence formation of intention

---

[43] Donald Dennett, *Brainstorms: Philosophical Essays on Mind and Psychology*, (Cambridge: The MIT Press, 1961), 301.

[44] Dennett, 301.

as well as beliefs. He correlatively suggests that "assent" is stronger than "desire." When an individual desires something, after an accumulation of various opinions on that something, the individual may come to believe and then assent to the system of opinions which have accumulated into a structure that motivates the individual to construct a belief state. Hartry Field says that

> the belief relation is a composite of two other relations: first, a relation between a person and a *sentence* that the person understands; second, a relation between the sentence and a set of possible worlds.[45]

In this network of beliefs, desire, attitudes, intentions, motivations, intuitions, feelings, possible worlds—all the raw materials of one's interior life as expressed in a piece of writing or expressed in speaking (in/direct quotation, conversation) and thinking (interior monologue)—intention is formed.

The Machine Analogy

The working of the brain has been successfully, provocatively, compared to a machine, specifically a computer, complete with its own multiple triggers, internal indicators and language. In fact, computer specialists are trying to create a computer which can think for itself like a human brain, the veritable "Hal" of the movie "2001" fame.

I would like to address here these issues of the computer metaphor and internal indicators as another avenue to a better understanding of how the brain works and how the mind forms intentions.

After the random forces gather themselves into some kind of pre-verbal network, there is what has been called an internal indicator or a trigger which issues then in words and behaviours. Fred Dretske uses the examples of the furnace, the frog, the finger and the trip to Minnesota to illustrate the existence of this internal indicator.

---

[45] Field, "Mental Representation," 80.

38

Many of us would say that the cause of our doing something or the reason we made a certain decision to do something is outside of ourselves; some other person or situation caused us to say or do something. Dretske's examples show that causes and reasons are triggered from or by something, a force, within the self, the furnace, the frog.

Most of us would say that the *cause*, the reason why, the room is warm is because the furnace is on. But Dretske twists the idea of cause and effect around such that causes and effects are dependent upon the internal workings of the furnace. There is a thermometer in the furnace which is the cause of the furnace going on when the temperature in the room dips too low. It is this "internal indicator"[46] that is the cause of the room being heated; of course, this is related to the temperature dipping too low but if the internal indicator were not there, the temperature could dip as low as it pleased to no effect.

Similarly, the manner in which a frog catches flies in order to feed and sustain itself is through an "internal fly indicator" which signals where the flies are and causes the frog's instinctual tongue movements. In terms of a human person's intentional structure, external circumstances (like the coldness in the room or the presence of the fly to the frog) touch some internal indicator in the person (which may or may not be present in others) which creates the internal state that issues in the spoken or written word or the behaviour. It is not an external set of circumstances *per se* that "causes" the reaction; it is the internal state that reacts to the external ones that "causes" a reaction. Awareness of the internal belief and desire states, the internal triggers, indicates why intentions are formed as they are. External circumstances are received through the senses and processed by the internal indicators, the neurochemical transmitters and reactors. Often, there are no external circumstances, no sensory input, and individuals react to that absence. Or there are no internal indicators, no triggers, and individuals react to *that* absence.

"The movement of my finger stands to my moving it something like the way *getting* to Minnesota stands to *going* to Minnesota. Though one hasn't *gone*

---

[46] Fred Dretske, "Why Thinking Helps," unpublished manuscript, 19.

to Minnesota unless one *gets* there, the going gets underway well before the arrival."[47]

I don't want to focus on the finger moving because that may be partly an unconscious reflex action, a muscle action, like the doctor tapping the knee cap with his instruments, but Dretske's example of getting to Minnesota involves an intentional, interior trigger. Certainly the intention to go to Minnesota may have unconscious motives and subsets of intentions and desires; these unconscious motives, intentions, and desires are not like the reflex action of a muscle moving a finger. I wish to differentiate intention–formation from simple neurochemistry. Certainly intention–formation can be wholly unconscious, but I shall discuss this later with regard to a "murder with no motive" scenario. An internal indicator registers the desire and forms the intention to go to Minnesota and the process of getting there is the external, behavioural enactment of the intention and desire motivating it. I believe that the frog, the furnace, the finger and the trip are excellent examples of my view of the intentional structure because the frog would not catch the fly, the furnace would not go on, the finger would not raise, the trip would not be undertaken and, by extension, the words would not be spoken, nor texts written, nor behaviours executed if there were not some "internal indicator" or series of internal indicators to trigger, motivate and, in some sense, intend that activity. Something within triggers the desire to speak or write words which will represent and communicate an intentional state or structure. And when the individual hears the words spoken or sees the words written, an internal indicator again is triggered which attests to the truth or falsity of the verbal propositions there. Kenneth Bruffee, quoting Jerome Bruner, notes:

> Infants can learn how to affect their surroundings . . . , he says, because their minds are equipped even in infancy with a "hypothesis generator" that gives them the ability to "form either higher order action routines or more generalized 'cognitive maps' of their world."[48]

---

[47] Dretske, "Why Thinking Helps," 15.

[48] Kenneth Bruffee, *Collaborative Learning: Higher Education, Interdependence and the Authority of Knowledge*, (Baltimore: The Johns Hopkins University Press, 1993), 161.

Jerry Fodor, Lynne Baker, and others have elaborated the analogy between the structure of a brain and a computer. Jerry Fodor's article, "Private Language, Public Languages" is one of the more well-ordered, clear presentations of the analogy. The internal workings of the mind have captured the imagination; and analogies like a computer or machine comparison are expected.

Fodor's view is that "you can't learn a language unless you already *know* one"[49] and he uses to great advantage the analogy that "real computers characteristically use at least two different languages: an input/output language in which they communicate with their environment and a machine language in which they talk to themselves (i.e., in which they run their computations)."[50] The point is that, though the machine must have a compiler if it is to use the input/output langauge, it doesn't *also* need a compiler for the machine language. What avoids an infinite regression of compilers is the fact that the machine is *built* with its own internal language. Roughly, the machine language differs from the input/output language in that its formulae correspond directly to relevant physical states and computational operations of the machine: the physics of the machine thus guarantees that the sequences of states and operations it runs through in the course of its computations respect the semantic constraints of the formulae in its internal language.

I want to focus here on what Fodor calls this "'one-stage regress' viz., from the natural language, the input-output language, to the internal code, the machine language. We can imagine an organism, a brain, which is born speaking whatever language its nervous system uses for computing."[51] Fodor reiterates that he wants to continue to rely quite heavily on the machine analogy "as an existence proof for devices which don't speak the language they compute in."[52] He summarises Wittgenstein in support of his point:

---

[49] Jerry A. Fodor, "Private Language, Public Languages," in *The Language of Thought*, (New York: Thomas Y. Cromwell Company, 1975), 61, 65.

[50] Fodor, 65-66.

[51] Fodor, 68.

[52] Fodor, 68.

> Wittgenstein has, in this respect, two ways of characterizing a private language: either as one whose terms refer to things that only its speaker can experience or as a language for the applicability of whose terms there exist no public criteria (or rules, or conventions). . . . If I am the only one who can know what a term like "mild tickle" refers to, then, clearly, the conventions for applying that term cannot be public. For, by hypothesis, only I could tell when the conventions are satisfied; only I would know whether a certain event is of the kind that falls under the conventions.[53]

Fodor's point is that even in the case of public languages which purport to represent and refer to a stable relation between the terms used and the way the world *is*: what is required is a stable relation between the way the terms are used and *the way the speaker believes the world to be.* Frank Smith, in his theory of the world in the mind, with regard to reading and writing, makes exactly the same point. Two of Smith's books articulate clearly, readably, this theory which Fodor and Wittgenstein, and I, am attempting to congeal. Smith calls it a "theory of the world in the mind" from which, through which and by which individuals understand what they read and are able to write sentences. (See my list of references for the specific citations.)

Fodor stresses the obvious fact that events will have physical descriptions complete with causal laws as well as psychological descriptions which explain, compute, the steps that the psychological organism took from stimulus to response. This is basically the process of the neurochemical transmissions and the biological-physical-chemical structure of the brain itself as elaborated in Restak's book *The Mind.* Fodor quotes Dennett (1969) in this regard:

> It is possible, perhaps, that the brain has developed storage and transmission methods involving syntactically analyzable events or structures, so that, for example, some patterns of molecules or impulses could be brain-word tokens, but even if there were some such 'language' or 'code' . . . there would also have to be mechanisms for 'reading' and

---

[53] Fodor, 69.

'understanding' this language. Without such mechanisms, the storage and transmission of sentence-like things in the brain . . . these reading mechanisms, in turn, would have to be information processing systems, and what are we to say of their internal states and events? Do *they* have syntactically analyzable parts? The regress must end eventually with some systems which store, transmit and process information in non-syntactic form . . . . this assumes that the nervous system is issuing commands which must be 'read' and translated into actions (or, anyhow, muscle contractions) by some *further* system that intervenes between the efferent nerves and the effectors. But this picture is no part of the theory. On the contrary, what is required is just that the *causal* properties of such physical events as are interpreted as messages in the internal code must be compatible with the *linguistic* properties that the interpretation assigns to those events.[54]

Fodor continues with three assumptions: the computational states ascribable to organisms can be directly explicated as relations between the organism and its *formulae*, its internal code. If the organism, the brain, can store information, then the organism must be in computational relation to the formula, the code, the language, which can translate what is stored. The second assumption is that the relations between the organism and its code are extremely close, narrow, fine-grained, i.e. highly technical and detailed. Thirdly, for every verbal proposition created by that organism by its code there will be the corresponding computational relationship between the code and the grammar of a particular language. The organism has a relation to the proposition, the code, and the computation of the proposition and its code into a language. Lynne Baker also talks about the machine analogy in her book *Saving Belief* in Chapter Three where she says that the "computer metaphor has spawned one of the most promising approaches to a science of the mind: functionalism."[55] She reinforces the more lucrative aspects of the machine analogy which maps the brain as a

---

[54] Fodor, 74.

[55] Lynne Rudder Baker, *Saving Belief: A Critique of Physicalism*, (Princeton University Press, 1987), 43.

kind of corporate entity, made up of various departments performing complex mental functions.

As Phenomenological Object

In an article, Rolf von Eckartsberg develops Baker's functionalist approach and employs a map as a metaphor for consciousness rather than a computer. He then proceeds to summarise the different theoretical paradigms or charts of various theorists who have attempted "to map consciousness." The form or structure which he gives to consciousness, to what I am calling in this chapter, the intentional structure, is of a "territory that can be mapped."[56]

> Psychological theory conceptualizes the existential process in a particular way by identifying, naming, selecting and interconnecting essential process-features as an interdependent network of constructs.[57]

I wish to extend the computer/machine analogy and consider intentional structures as phenomenological objects that can be mapped, structured and studied but in terms of the foregoing comments in the previous chapter that intentional structures, because of the neurochemical workings of the brain, continually deconstruct themselves.

Rolf von Eckartsburg includes intentionality under a subsection of a chapter of his book entitled *Existential-Phenomenological Field-Psychology*, where he says that

> through the insight that there is an essential *intentional structure* of consciousness and all conscious acts, *intentionality* became articulated. Intentionality refers to the fact that consciousness is always consciousness of something which is not consciousness itself, but a meaning for consciousness . . . . The key insight of phenomenology is that human meaning

---

[56] Rolf von Eckartsberg, "Maps of the Mind: The Cartography of Consciousness," in *The Metamorphosis of Consciousness*, (New York: Plenum Press, 1981), 22.

[57] Eckartsberg, 23.

and encounter *connect* person and world, subject and objects and establishes a relation *in between.*[58]

The consciousness then is a consciousness of the fact that there are intentional structures. Stephen Stich's "syntactic theory of mind" says that

> cognitive states . . . can be systematically mapped to abstract syntactic objects in such a way that causal interactions among cognitive states, as well as causal links with stimuli and behavioural events, can be described in terms of the syntactic properties and relations of the abstract objects to which the cognitive states are mapped.[59]

A "formality condition" is established as part of the "computational theory of mind," in contradistinction to a grammatical or syntactic, which urges that "mental processes have access only to formal (nonsemantic) properties of the mental representations over which they are defined."[60] The neurochemical activity occurring in the brain, comparable to the electrical, computational activity in a computer, gives it its "form."

On the other hand, a syntactic, as opposed to computational-formal theory, suggests ways that the computations in the brain which give it its form have a "syntax" that can be "mapped," using words, the tools of language and rhetoric, perceived and understood by others. The formal-computational theory focuses more on the internal, 'nonsemantic (non-syntactic)' processes or forces, as I am calling them, before any "mapping" is done. That is,

> mental states must be individuated according to their role within the individual, without regard to their relations to an environment . . . . The causal relations between mental states have to be connected to the semantic and syntactic relations between representations, whether the causal relations parallel rational or irrational semantic and syntactic relations.[61]

---

[58] Eckartsberg, 46.

[59] Devitt, "Why Fodor Can't Have It Both Ways," unpublished manuscript, 1.

[60] Devitt, 1.

[61] Devitt, 1, 28.

Edmund Husserl's "phenomenological bracket" relates to these conceptions of a syntactic, grammatic and a computational-formal theory of mind. Essentially, Husserl wishes to view and study the activity of a mind, a consciousness, as a phenomenon, a "formal" object in its own right and the major tool that he uses for this study is the "bracket,"[62] the device through which the individual consciousness forms and expresses itself and so it can be studied as an object in itself. The phenomenological bracket is formed when the conscious mind sifts through the multiple sense perceptions, the "hyletic" materials, as Husserl calls them,[63] that have accumulated. As the individual becomes involved in more and more life experiences (behaviours) generally, these hyletic materials (received perceptual-sense experiences) accumulate (register) in consciousness (unconsciousness, subconsciousness, pre-consciousness) and from these accumulated materials, the conscious mind intentionally "brackets" its understanding of itself, or part of itself, and its particular experiences. Husserl's phenomenology contributes to an understanding of how intentions are formed to the extent that his theory says that the workings of the mind, the consciousness itself, are a "phenomenal" object of study as is any other phenomenal object in nature.

The syntactic theory of mind parallels Husserl's suggestion that there is an immense network (a syntax) of perceptual, raw materials from which individuals bracket, formally organise, correlate and compute their own understandings of particular experiences, which process parallels the formal-computational theory, and this syntax is the deep structure of Chomsky's transformational grammar.

The intentional structure in consciousness, then, is syntactic, layered. What I am interested in noting here is the "formal" activity, the interior act of forming intentions, that occurs before any behavioural or verbal execution is performed. Individuals, like archaeologists and paleontologists, read the neurochemical traces and connections, one uncovering another or interconnecting with another.

---

[62] Edmund Husserl, *Ideas: General Introduction to Phenomenology*, (New York: Collier Books, 1931), 91 ff.

[63] Husserl, 91, 94, 105, 114, 226-227, 230, 292.

"Intentionality [was] the mark that sunder[ed] the universe in the most fundamental way: dividing the mental from the physical."[64] The "mental" which is said to be divided from the "physical" in this quotation is the conscious, unconscious, subconscious, preconscious intentional structure of the mind and the "physical" consists of the verbal and behavioural structures which emerge therefrom. But, this is a

> heavy load to bear. . . connecting the intentional domain . . . to the non-intentional domain of the physical sciences . . . . Language is without a doubt the crowning achievement of evolution, an achievement that feeds on itself to produce ever more versatile and subtle relational systems.[65]

In other words, to study mental activity and intentional states, conscious, subconscious, preconscious intentional structures as separate objects in themselves is quite literally impossible. They can only be accessed in their expression in behaviour, speech or writing, and writing is the "crowning achievement" of those expressions.

The only ways that I can discover what another person is thinking, feeling, intending, desiring or believing about anything, the individual's intentional structure, in particular, is to hear the individual speak or read something that the individual wrote or watch the individual behave, which activities are based upon those desires, beliefs, intentions etc. or the absence thereof. To be sure, individuals can speak and act and in so doing clearly, unambiguously, reveal intentional structure and stance. Their knowledge of physics, chemistry, biology, science or history can be evidenced in their speech and writing, but I may not discover "why" the person decided to learn history, science or philosophy as they did. The "intentional stance" is "the possession of certain information and supposing it to be directed by certain goals."[66]

---

[64] Donald Dennett, *Brainstorms*, 22.

[65] Dennett, 17.

[66] Dennett, 6.

"We want to assign intrinsically representational entities to mental states to serve as contents"[67] which are defined as "S-propositions assigned to an intentional, mental state."[68] This a key distinction, as I understand it, for my purposes here. That is, when a sentence is written which proposes to communicate a particular mental-intentional state, the sentence not only expresses a "trace" of the content of the state but also serves then as an Husserlean objectification of the state. In other words, I express the content of my mental state, in a syntactic-grammatical way, a verbal structure, a grammatical-rhetorical structure, and then I examine that content as a separate, Husserlean, phenomenological, formal object. Similarly, I can express the content of a "trace" of my intentional structure in a behavioural way, without words, and I can then return to examine that behaviour, verbalise it, in language.

"Assigning uninterpreted sentences to mental states and assigning interpretations of those sentences"[69] is a crucial distinction. As I see it, when I wish to communicate my mental state, my intentions etc. through a verbal structure, I am actually performing another activity, the activity of interpreting and re-translating myself, my own interior sentences, states and the generative forces which make up my intentional structure. As I come to formulate "uninterpreted sentences" in consciousness which I believe will express my intentional state, I arrange them in such a way that I am assigning interpretations to them.

And this is Derrida's point: the moment that this sentence, as a proposition, is constructed, spoken or written, it becomes something "other," an object that, when examined, expresses only a "trace" of the true "contents" of the mental, intentional state.

The question is: does the syntax of the verbal and behavioural structures which individuals perform represent, at least minimally, the traces, the rhetorical-grammatical structure of the intentional structure of the mind from which they came? It is "plausible to claim that there is a fairly general parallelism be-

---

[67] Hartry Field, "Critical Notice: Robert Stalnaker, *Inquiry*," *Philosophy of Science*, September, 1986, Volume 53, #3, 426-27.

[68] Hartry Field, "Stalnaker on Intentionality," *Pacific Philosophical Quarterly*, April 1986, Volume 67, #2, 98.

[69] Field, "Critical Notice: Robert Stalnaker, *Inquiry*," 433.

48

tween the complexity of belief states and systems and the complexity of the sentences that expresses them."[70]

Hartry Field says that it is his own strategy, apparently much like Robert Stalnaker's, whom Field was critiquing,

> to assume that mental states of believing, desiring, and so forth could be given a roughly sentential structure . . . an attractive feature of this way of viewing things [Stalnaker's] is that many of the features which have been argued to be essential to a plausible theory of reference are features that clearly have to enter in to any explanation of why my written words or utterances are reliable indicators of both the external and internal worlds.[71]

Sentences uttered in speech and writing or behaviours performed contain or express propositions which explain intention and were formed and motivated by the intentional structuring of interior forces. The sentences uttered or constructed or behaviours performed are the result of the individual's interior process of self-translation and self-interpretation of a multiplicity of intersecting, random forces called beliefs, desires, attitudes, and feelings from which the person chooses (or often is compelled unconsciously) to focus and so place as central in the articulation of the argument, the explanation of the behaviour, the formation of the intention, in the sentential structure. These individuals foreground certain beliefs, desires and attitudes and groups of beliefs, desires, attitudes as "states," as more significant than others, as primary, or as a way to replace others or fill gaps where individuals perceive that certain beliefs, desires or attitudes should be present.

Husserl's natural standpoint which parallels but is quite different from Derrida's natural attitude is what Lawrence Watson calls a "phenomenological attitude."[72] The Husserlean phenomenological attitude, according to Watson, is

---

[70] Jerry A. Fodor, "Propositional Attitudes," in *Readings in Philosophy of Psychology*, Volume 2, edited by Ned Block, (Harvard University Press, 1981), 52.

[71] Field, "Critical Notice: Robert Stalnaker, *Inquiry*," 436, 439

[72] Lawrence Watson, "Understanding a Life History as a Subjective Document: Hermeneutical and Phenomenological Perspectives," (*Ethos*, 1976, Volume 4), 99.

an "introspective protocol," which examines the contents of consciousness, the raw materials there, and constructs a "portrait" of that consciousness, an intentional structure. The construct is the Husserlean "bracket."

Derrida and Husserl part company here. Derrida would hardly settle for a particular construct of consciousness as an explanation or statement of intention. The natural attitude is one which continually deconstructs in an interactive freeplay of unconscious, preconscious and subconscious intersections and traces. Husserlean constructs and brackets can and will indeed be formed, constructed and articulated to explain behaviour and intentions but must be continually deconstructed as new information is received and processed. The constructive process, the process of generating the language (the grammar, syntax and rhetoric), or the behaviour, the structure with which to express intentions, attitudes, ideas is the natural impulse for Husserl because it affords individuals some opportunity to express and consequently understand themselves as objects, as phenomena, as persons who form intentions based upon some kind of structure or lack of structure.

These amorphous, free-ranging, primitive illocutionary forces interact as they do, until which time the person stops and interprets some of them and this interpretation involves the Chomskean transformation, self-translation, into a grammar, an Husserlean construct which will successfully communicate them to others. Individuals then use the conventions of their own language grammars and dialects with which to communicate successfully to others the range of these illocutionary forces at work in them. The construction of sentences as propositions which express a particular force is a process of separating and privileging that particular force or locus of forces over others which are in continual interaction. This process I shall consider in more detail in Chapter Three. The person attempts to construct other sentences which will frame the other forces and the person will attempt to situate these in a nexus of relations which will serve to explain how and why a particular intention was formed and a behaviour executed.

The key, central moment in this process is the self-interpretation and the transformation of illocutionary forces into a structure or system with which the person is comfortable. This initial transformation and interpretation of neurochemical impulses that I am calling "forces" involves the compilation and configuration of a series of disjointed, illogical, mental fragments: incomplete sentences, disjointed, disorganised thoughts, blanks; the forces continue to interact while the person tries to hold them in check by making them into complete sentences which join and organise into a coherent intentional structure.

Eventually some form of a complete argument or explanation consisting of a (hopefully) logical series of sentences succeeds in explaining specific behaviours and intentions. I will show in Chapter Three how these locutions in the speech or pieces of writing can be traced back to the free-ranging illocutionary forces and how the verbal structure also evidences the gaps and deletions, many of which are inaccessible anyway because they have been etched in the unconscious, preconscious mind and have not been neurochemically "ignited" as yet but may be at some future time.

A significant part of this self-transforming, self-translating process, for oneself and then for others, particularly with regard to intention formation, is the creation of the language which will successfully do so. Individuals use the tools and structures of their own languages to communicate the various levels of forces that make up their intentional structure. According to Derrida, such communication is virtually impossible since these forces are always in motion and process. To stop them is not only a violence but an impossibility, an act of imagination, a fiction. When controversial behaviour is explained or intentions are defended, the clarity with which the individual traces the interrelation of primitive, illocutionary forces through use of logical transition and reference is helpful then in understanding behaviour and intention and communicating these to others.

Either before or after a particular controversial action is performed or word uttered, individuals have the opportunity to examine the range of primitive, illocutionary forces available to them and so group those forces in a way that is satisfactory, explanatory, to them. This process of examination and grouping is a discursive, conversational one among the many voices within individuals. Eventually, individuals decrease the discursive interaction and begin to privilege some of the elements, some forces, over others and so act or speak according to these grouped forces.

By way of conclusion to this second chapter on the interior structure, I would like to refer again to Eckartsberg's mapping. He speaks about "inner time consciousness"[73] in his introductory chapter. This is an important consideration for my analysis of intention formation because in this realisation that for consciousness, for the various intersections and neurochemical transmissions and firings there, the creation of time and the presence of space have little relation to the neurochemical firings and interconnections, traces and realisations, intention formation. Activity in the mind can be considered in terms of physical space in the sense that it is induced by external sensory experiences from outside space into the biochemical firings of the internal space in the composition of the brain itself as fixed in the skull; experiences of hearing, taste, touch, smell, sight etc. locate themselves in a particular external space. That is, the body and the brain occupy spaces, and the particular sense is stimulated in the realm of that physical space.

Philosophers like Eckartsberg and Derrida insist that the actual activity of processing in the mind is removed from the particular time (day, hour, week, month, year etc.) and space (body, earth) and assigns time and space to the experience. The mind can make the experience longer than the number of actual external seconds that ticked away. An experience may have taken ten minutes but I may reflect on it for as many minutes as I choose. The mind can take the experience that occurred in a particular place (space) and transfer it to another place (space). Time and space are not completely imposed on the mind from the outside. Eckartsberg uses Ernest Keen's (1975) cognitive map of being a self in time as his example and the map is reminiscent of Freud's mystic writing pad or DeQuincey's palimpsest.

> The experience of being a self in time is quite complex. Right now I have a sense of myself. What is involved in that sense of self? In the figure, I remember my childhood (1), and I anticipate that I shall die (2). When I was a child, I anticipated finding a job (3). My memory of how I anticipated finding a job (5) compared to my memory of finding a job (4), and it either lived up to my expectations, or I am somehow disappointed. I made retirement plans when I found my job (6). I now remember making them (7) and now make new ones (8). I shall look back at having done all that (9),

---

[73] Eckartsberg, 47.

and, as I am dying, I shall remember looking back (10). I now anticipate how I shall remember the retirement plans that I am making now (11). Not all of these horizons are equally important for how I understand myself in my job. But they are all implicitly part of my understanding. Occasionally one of them becomes crucial, as does my notion that when I retire I shall be amazed at how stupid my earlier retirement plans were. Part of my motivation for changing them now is that I do not want to look back and see myself as having been stupid (12). This process is anticipating remembering an anticipation (13). The diagram is complex enough to indicate how complex being a self in time really is. It is also clear that the diagram is much too simple; had I thrown in my marriage, the births of my children, the marriages of my children, my earlier physical abilities, their current decrease, and their eventual deterioration, and the hundreds of other issues that are important in my sense of myself, the diagram would have become unwieldy.[74]

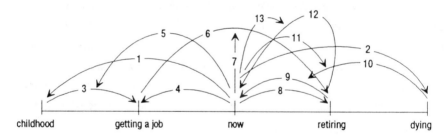

What individuals experience in a particular present moment makes its sundry traces and these may then intersect in new and different ways in future "present moments" and become forces in intentional structuring. Neurochemical brain activity in the multiple levels of conscious-unconscious and subconscious intersections is in a Derridean process of an "always already" continuous present and the neurochemical activity of the brain and body constantly records the hyletic, perceptual experiences of the senses. The fact of the matter is that these neurotransmitted connections constantly intersect in a continuous activity

---

[74] Eckartsberg, 48-49.

in a continuous present which consciousness then names "past" experiences, which have been buried in unconscious, subconscious, preconscious mind. The present activity of consciousness becomes then this "thick present"[75] of ongoing intersections.

There is, in effect, no "state" of consciousness, as in a mental state, an Husserlean "bracket," because activity in the brain never freezes into a "state;" it is always actively charging, discharging and interconnecting. It is part of what I am calling "forming intentions" when the mind creates the "states." Consciousness constructs itself; consciousness constructs its own intentional systems of beliefs and desires based upon this thick accumulation of perceptions. Derrida says that these constructions must be continually deconstructed as new input is continually added with the continual firing of the neurotransmitters in the mind.

Eckartsberg's chapter is sprinkled with diagrams like Keen's which construct the mind in terms of geometric shapes like triangles, cylinders, ovals or concentric circles and he elaborates these diagrams with an accompanying prose text explaining the theories of consciousness of Assgioli, Wilber, Tart, Rosenstock-Huesey, Keen, Freud, Lewin and Swami Rama which the diagrams represent. My point in making reference to Eckartsberg's map at the end of this chapter, especially Eckartsberg's reference to Keen, is to illustrate the fact that the consciousness which forms intentions and executes behaviours is adrift amidst a sea of perceptions which it then brackets into intentional systems applicable to certain behaviours and then deconstructs these into another system for another behaviour in another circumstance.

> *One of the Fathers, in great severity, called poesy* vinum daemonum *because it fills the imagination; and yet it is but with the shawdow of a lie. But it is not the lie that passeth through the mind, but the lie that sinketh and settleth in it, that doth hurt.*

> Francis Bacon, "Of Truth," 1625

---

[75] Jean-Jacques Mayoux, "Variations on the Time-Sense in *Tristram Shandy*," in Laurence Sterne *Tristram Shandy: An Authoritative Text, The Author of the Novel, Criticism.* Edited by Howard Anderson. (New York: W.W. Norton and Company, 1980), 578.

CHAPTER THREE

The Verbal / Behavioural Structures

*Words and deeds are quite indifferent modes
of the divine energy. Words are also actions,
and actions are a kind of words.*

Ralph Waldo Emerson, *Essays*, xiii

In Chapter One, I distinguished the intentional, verbal and behavioural structures as a gestalt of relational foci of importance, each world having its own internal nexus of elements. In Chapter Two, I focused more closely on the interior, intentional states, and in this chapter I would like to focus on the verbal structures, the language and rhetoric, and the attendant behavioural structures, as constructs which are rooted in the intentional state. Later, I shall focus on specific verbal structures, narratives explicating specific behaviours from the writings of Thomas DeQuincey, Geoffrey Chaucer, Graham Greene, and Henry Fielding.

Here I focus on the exterior world of words and behaviours, thereby making those worlds primary, and in so doing I will locate the nexus of elements in those structures which are constituted, rooted in and are really only traces of the complex intentional world. I will execute this focus in this chapter in predominantly two ways:

First, I will consider Noam Chomsky's theory of transformational grammar along with Charles Chastain's reflections on referentiality, and then I will consider speech act theory's distinction between constative and performative illocutionary acts and John Searle's comments on referentiality.

Then I shall consider two sections of two literary texts, Flannery O'Connor's *The Violent Bear It Away* and Graham Greene's *Monsignor Quixote* as examples of the theory considered first.

The truth seems to be that any contentions about intentional mental states and activities are a complicated network of biochemical intersections resulting in the creation of numerous intentional systems based on any number of these intersections in conscious, unconscious, preconscious, subconscious mind and the individual participates in an activity that I call "self-translation" in forming intentions and executing behaviour.

I now wish to proceed to examine more carefully how these "primitive illocutionary forces," as speech act theorist John Searle calls them, which result in an innate, machine-like, "language of thought," are articulated or acted out.

With G.E.M. Anscombe, I ask "What went on in the mind and issued in the action? . . . what produced this [particular] action or thought or feeling . . . what did you see or hear or feel, or what ideas or images cropped up in your mind and led up to it?"[1] The intention is what is aimed for or chosen, whereas the motive is the drive behind the intention. Motives determine choices and hence, intentions are separate objects from motives and desires which function as determiners or causes for the intentions or desires.[2]

I will pursue the key issues here of the internal causality in the mind in terms of the images "cropping up" there, which activity results in external, often randomly associated actions and words, and I will discuss them in terms of the motives or drives that propel individuals to intend particular courses of action or goals, to make certain choices, to articulate certain words.

When the conscious mind attempts to articulate the interior, mental activity of intention-formation through language (speech and/or writing), another entirely new interior, mental process is occurring: the language act which creates the verbal structure which analyses a behaviour in fact is a behaviour in and of itself. The language is used either to defend a behaviour that was already performed or to explain the mental processes leading to the intention to perform

---

[1] G.E.M. Anscombe, *Intention*, (New York: Cornell University Press, 1969), 17-18.

[2] Anscombe, 18-19.

a behaviour, perhaps controversial or questionable, at a later time. By controversial, I mean against the law of society or one's conscience.

Stephen Schiffer's "strong language of thought hypothesis" says that "we think in an internal system of representation."[3] And yet there is mental activity occurring before any internal system of representation is created; this pre-verbal activity is, to be sure, part of the structure of the internal system. Part of his hypothesis is that "propositional attitudes [relate] to sentences in one's language of thought."[4] Chomsky's theory is that the language, the rhetoric produced, evidences this generative, transformative process by which those internal sentences are created and made into a language.

In *Brainstorms*, Donald Dennett writes that

> the system of representations must have a generative grammar. That is, the system must be such that you understand the system and know the finite vocabulary you can generate the representations—the sentences of brain-writing—you haven't yet examined.[5]

Schiffer comes closest to what I am trying to illustrate here when he quotes Harman: "It is plausible that our internal states of representation 'have elements and structure in a way that is analogous to the way in which sentences have elements and structure.'"[6]

The significant point here is that a particular written text articulating intentional states, explaining and defending behaviours, (or the words as behaviours themselves) may be read and studied as Husserlean phenomenological objects, formulaic-computational structures, analogous to the internal, syntactic state. But, on the other hand, in keeping with Derrida's trace theory, this written text (its sentences and formal structure) is syntactically analogous to the complex

---

[3] Stephen Schiffer, "Truth and the Theory of Content,"in *Meaning and Understanding*, edited by Herman Parret and Jacques Bouveresse (New York: Walter de Gruyter Publishers, 1981), 208.

[4] Schiffer, 207.

[5] Donald Dennett, *Brainstorms: Essays on Mind and Psychology*, (Cambridge: The MIT Press, 1961), 42.

[6] Schiffer, 207.

of interactions only to the extent that it is itself syntactically complicated with multiple threads, braids, interlaces, sub-texts, stories within stories, figures of speech and images.

Brentano's "nexus of exemplification" asserts that there are entities (propositions expressing desires, beliefs and their states; call them a, b, c, . . . n) which form connections (call them A, B, C, . . . N), which connections can then be considered as entities again forming new, other systems of interrelations, nexi of exemplification.

The formation of a sentence in the mind, the content of which sentence is *about the mind and its intentional structure*, is first of all a separate, different mental activity from the utterance of a sentence which is motivated by the intentional structure, and after these sentences are constructed, they become phenomenological objects whereby the persons who created them realise that there are many other sentences that might be added to it or that can replace it in order to explain and/or represent adequately the intentional activity. And so sentences become Derridean traces in the sense that no amount of sentences ever really capture or represent the intentional structure.

It seems to me that the problem of a rhetoric for a formation of intention rests on the horns of the Derridean-Husserlean dilemma, the construction-deconstruction controversy. Words and behaviours are constituted in the intentional structure, and the words, behaviours and structures have the potential to be examined and analysed and ideally re-formed. Language is an effective, organisational tool in this examination and appropriate rhetoric clarifies.

Fred Dretske, in *Explaining Behaviours*, gives what he considers to be the "essence of the mental" when he says that

> a very important fact about representational systems . . . [is that they give] content a fine-grainedness that is characteristic of intentional systems. [They] make verbal expressions of their content *intensional* rather than *extensional*. It is this feature, together with the system's capacity for misrepresentation and the reference or aboutness of its elements, that many philosophers regard as the essence of the mental.[7]

---

[7] Dretske, *Explaining Behaviours: Reasons in a World of Causes*, (Cambridge, Mass: MIT Press, 1988), 75.

I interpret "intensional" here to mean the "fine-grained," as in pre-verbal, neurochemical, detailed activity of the mind which comprises that complex, pre-verbal network of attitudes, intentions, feelings, desires, beliefs etc. which become "extensional" in the verbal, coarse-grained articulation and expression of them in speech, writing or behaviour.

Hartry Field defines coarse-grained propositions as a set of possible world propositions and fine-grained propositions as a certain complicated kind of function defined out of possible worlds.[8] I pointed out in Chapter Two that Field, in his April, 1986 article on Stalnaker's book *Inquiry*, re-asserts that his strategy in the article "Mental Representation" is to assume that mental, intentional states of believing, desiring, and so forth could be given a roughly sentential structure, and then to impose on those states a componential ('computational') semantics which specified truth conditions for sentences with analogous structures.[9] He wants to give a "materialistically adequate account of believing, desiring, and so forth."[10]

Which is what I wish to do and is my key point in this chapter. I wish to consider the possibility that certain written texts or speeches can be "materialistically adequate accounts" of various intentional states and structures of the writer or speaker. Words and behaviours are motivated by interior states. Words which analyse those words and behaviours constituted in those interior states are also motivated there. The "sentential, syntactic structure" of a written text represents in a computational-formal way the various, but with Derrida certainly not all, mental states of believing, desiring, etc.

G.E.M. Anscombe articulates what she feels to be the central problem in her work on intentionality:

> . . . intention itself can be complete, although it remains a purely interior thing. All this conspires to make us think that if we want to know a man's intentions it is into the contents of his mind, and only into these, that we must enquire . . .

---

[8] Field, "Mental Representation," in *Readings in Philosophy and Psychology*, Volume Two, edited by Ned Block (Harvard University Press, 1981), 81.

[9] Field, "Mental Representation," 104-105.

[10] Field, "Mental Representation," 81.

60

[However,] mental causality is itself characterised by being known without observation."[11]]

Once the conscious mind decides to express, analyse or represent its intentional structures, it looks for ways to do so and these ways usually result in spoken words or particular actions. But substantive intentional states can also be expressed in silence and reclusivity, inaction.

When individuals decide to articulate their intentional structure, how they form or formed intentions, in speech or writing; when they decide to communicate why they said, did or spoke a certain series of actions, words or behaviours; or why they did not speak or act; they seek a language with which to express this.

With Chomsky, Richard Ohmann says that each person has this language, an innate language, discourse, a conversation, occurring at a pre-verbal stage, at the level of neurochemical transmissions and accumulations, impulses, compulsions, forces, and part of the brain, part of consciousness, if you like, decides that it will undertake the mental activity by which it will try to represent some of this continuous discourse but of course in a discontinuous, discrete language.[12]

Transformational "Rhetoric" and "Innate Language"

Noam Chomsky's transformational grammar assumes Ohmann's assertion that there is this internal discourse occurring and this discourse must be in some kind of a language that is "innate"[13] to the individual. This innate language is not something that is taught from the outside. It is similar to Lynne Baker and Jerry Fodor's computer language analogy and each individual has a unique "map of consciousness," using Eckartsburg's metaphor. What is taught in school (from the outside) is the ability to communicate the content of the mind co-operatively through

---

[11] Anscombe, 9, 24.

[12] Richard Ohmann, "Speech Acts and the Definition of Literature," *Philosophy and Rhetoric*, 4 (1971), 1.

[13] Noam Chomsky, Hilary Putnam and Nelson Goodman, "Symposium on Innate Ideas," *The Philosophy of Language*, edited by John Searle, (Oxford University Press, 1971).

the conventional language structures and systems and social-behavioural tools of the particular society and culture.

But individuals have the capacity to construct first their own language systems, a capacity which is built into the structure of the brain itself, but that language system must be translated, "transformed," as Chomsky suggests, into a language that is accessible, acceptable, first to the individual and then communicable to others. The structures of motivation and intention in consciousness, the discourse itself among random forces which interact forming intentions, attitudes, desires and motivations, must be transformed, translated, by the individual, into a visible structure of particular words and sentences of a particular language. Chomsky (and others) call this a "generative" process which I believe is another appropriate and effective term and image to explain the process here; there is a generator, a force, an unlocatable *energeia*, as Derrida writes, and "illocutionary" as Searle writes, which is a process of continuous activity that can be directed toward language acquisition and creation on its way to the expression of intention.

Illocutionary activity is the name given by speech act theorists to that generative process of producing locutions, words, sentences, speech. The generation of a language, or a behaviour, from the structures of forces in consciousness, to express the discursive activity in consciousness about a particular object, involves a generation of a language, a communicable structure of sentences and paragraphs, first for the individual and then for others so that individuals' intentional structures will be accessible to themselves and others.

In 1962, Noam Chomsky perceived that the "current issues in linguistic theory" rested with the arrival of a semantic methodology with which to categorise (taxonomise) and theorise (explain the motivation for) about the morphological (systematic, syntactic) and phonological (speech) structure of language.

In "A Transformational Approach to Syntax," he defines morphemes as "a relatively substantial classification of sounds;" morphemes are "certain classes of sequences of phonemes" and constituents are "certain classes of sequences of morphemes."[14] The clearer level of analysis of a sentence is in terms of

---

[14] Noam Chomsky, "A Transformational Approach to Syntax," in *The Structure of Language: Readings in the Philosophy of Language*, edited by Jerry A Fodor and Jerrold J. Katz, (New Jersey: Prentice-Hall, Inc., 1964), 212.

62

"phrase structure"[15] where the major noun phrase is separated from the verb phrase. His language theory seeks to define its linguistic theory in terms of a grammar for L for an arbitrary language L.[16] The "arbitrary" language is each person's own language.

"I murdered them because they were there," confesses a murderer. The sentence itself is a grammatical structure which is a transformation of an intentional structure and is also an expression of what happened in the external-behavioural world. The central, primary world of the Platonic "real" is the external-behavioural, the world of the murder itself. The verbal structuring of the events leading up to and surrounding the murder is at one remove from it and the intentional structure of the murderer is at a third remove.

The sentence, as a verbal structure in itself, not only has its own primary elements consisting of subjects and predicates ("I murdered" and "they were there") and a conjunction ("because"), but it also accesses to a certain extent the behavioural and intentional structures. Sentences need to be added to this sentence which would enlarge the intentional-behavioural structures. With the addition of more simple, compound, complex and compound-complex sentence arrangements, more access would be made available to the intentional structure of forces ("because they were there") in the murderer and external sequence of events in the behaviour ("I murdered").

In terms of transformational grammar and the innateness theory, the sentence, "I murdered them because they were there," explicates the primary activity of murder in the external behavioural forum. The events leading up to and surrounding the murder could be put into language as a sequence of elements in time and place to explain the sequence of events leading up to and following upon the murder. In terms of intentional structure of forces, the sentence explicates a primary force in the intentional structure. It is an admission by the murderer that "murder" is a primary force[17] within, which is surrounded by a gestalt of other forces that also need now to be verbalised.

[15] Chomsky, 223.

[16] Chomsky, 240.

[17] John Searle and Daniel Vanderveken, *The Foundations of Illocutionary Logic*, (Cambridge University Press, 1985), 1. John Searle and Daniel Vanderveken use this word "force" in

This interior-intentional force called "murder" in the verbal structure, which describes both the behaviour of murder in the external forum and the force of murder in the intentional structure, is both a noun and a verb[18] and is a noun and verb in the behavioural and intentional structures.

That is, as a noun, it can be the subject or object in a sentence. As a verb, it can be the sentence's predicate. In terms of the description of the external behaviour, it states the fact that the activity of murder occurred; a murder happened. The verbal structure has a referent outside of itself which referent is both an action ("to murder"—verb) and an event ("a murder"—noun). In terms of the description of the intentional structure of interior forces, it indicates, as a noun, that a state or gestalt of "murder" exists there. As a verb, it indicates that there is an activity called "murder" circulating in some particular nexus of an individual's particular intentional structure. The word "murder" of course invites explication and explanation of both the behaviour and the intention. The word "murder" in the verbal structure invites the participation and inclusion of other words, constructed into sentences, which describe and explain the nexus of external activity surrounding the murder. As an activity (verb) and state (noun) in the murderer, it invites further explication and explanation of the nexus of forces surrounding it; thus, a rhetoric for a formation of an intention to murder.

My point is that there is this nexus of forces within individuals which circulate around one another to form states, attitudes, dispositions which in turn circulate around each other. One particular nexus of forces forming a particular state is not the only one and because of the nature of the neurochemical activity in the brain, they are always circulating and re-arranging. The explication of the events leading up to and surrounding a murder is an explication of a behavioural structure that is fixed in time and space. It is possible that the language could communicate a fairly full picture of all the details with newer details added as they are discovered. But it is possible to exhaust all of the details because they occur in finite time and space. It is not possible to exhaust all of the

---

explaining the thing that motivates the speaking of particular words, and I am using it here as a word to explain the motivations and behaviours as well.

[18] Eric H. Lenneberg, "The Capacity for Language Acquisition," in *The Structure of Language: Readings in the Philosophy of Language*, edited by Jerry A. Fodor and Jerrold J. Katz, (New Jersey: Prentice-Hall, Inc., 1964), 9.

neurochemical transmissions because they occur constantly, infinitely, however fictional they may be in terms of the external reality.

The verbal structure, the language and rhetoric, cannot capture such a full, coherent portrait of the internal structure of intentional forces because they are in this constantly changing circularity, thus "temporary insanity;" the neurochemical impulses cannot be fixed in space and time like external, observable behaviours can and like verbal structures themselves can. The interior forces which group to form intentional states and systems are always in intersecting motion and therefore, according to Derrida, unreachable, untranslatable, inaccessible.

The internal gestalt of forces circulating around the primary force "murder" as expressed by the *word* "murder" is what I am calling examination and formation of intention. A portrait of these forces needs to be established which is in contextual integration with various external events and behaviours, which also need to be established in portraits of contextual integration. The relationship of the individual person to the formation, explanation or execution of each of these is central and crucial to the intentional structure, the verbal explanatory structure and the behavioural execution because only the individual can articulate the structures of each of these.[19]

Husserl, Chomsky and Ohmann contend that it is possible to access and bracket the activity of intention formation and innate languaging in a particular conventional language. Derrida would agree but he, no doubt, would say that the bracket needs to be deconstructed again because new information is always being transacted, even the new information of the bracketed material itself returns to the creator as something new. Innate language begins at this what one might call "baby-talk" level of pre-verbal discourse (gurgles, coos and groans) in the individual mind where these illocutionary forces circulating around various centers motivate, generate, and activate the creation of the language that will articulate the structures. The individual then translates this "language" into socially acceptable, understandable terms. According to H.P. Grice's co-operative principle, the individual is sincerely interested in communicating as clearly and concisely as possible all of the necessary information to the listener such

---

[19] Robert C. Stalnaker, *Inquiry*, (Cambridge, Mass.: MIT Press, 1984), 15.

that the listener or reader will understand the intentions. The writer or speaker does not want to confuse or obscure in any way.

The intentional structures are located in the circulation of these motivating forces at various centers and they drive or propel the person to organise and create belief and desire states and intentional structures with which the individual is comfortable and can behave comfortably; until which time the behaviour is uncomfortable or controversial in some way and the intentional structure needs to be explained and/or re-constructed.

The Husserlean hyletic, raw materials based upon sensory, experiential input which are recorded in the brain circulate around Derrida's inaccessible forces at centers of a conscious-unconscious-preconscious-subconscious matrix. There are an infinite variety of combinations of cognitive-emotive nexi in the right and left hemispheres. The intellectual-cognitive materials, felt to be left-brained activity, entail the logical formulations, syntheses and analyses. This activity tends to contain factual information that can be documented, correlated with other people's experiences. Beliefs, attitudes, ideas, facts, constructs, systems are formed here. The emotional-psychological formulations, on the other hand, in the right brain, juggle desires, motivations, feelings, and intuitions. Various emotional-psychological nexi of feelings become associated, it seems to me, with the illocutionary force behind a particular cognitive-intellectual stance.

Eric H. Lenneberg argues in "The Capacity for Language Acquisition" that there are ". . . highly specialized, biological propensities that shape the development of speech in the child and that roots of language may be as deeply grounded in our natural constitution as for instance a predisposition to use our hands."[20] All languages identify on approximately three points: phonology-phonetic systems, syntax and structure.[21] The existence of an innate impulse, an innate releasing mechanism,[22] for symbolic communication can hardly be ques-

---

[20] Eric H. Lenneberg, "The Capacity for Language Acquisition," in *The Structure of Language: Readings in the Philosophy of Language*, edited by Jerry A. Fodor and Jerrold J. Katz, (New Jersey: Prentice-Hall, Inc., 1964), 279.

[21] Lenneberg, 599-600.

[22] Lenneberg, 596.

66

tioned.[23] Transformational grammars allow speakers to exercise semantic, phonological, syntactic, interpretative talents. They give writers and speakers the tools with which to construct. In discourse analysis, the distributional relations between the sentences in the discourse are analysed and the analysis is correlated with the language of the social situation.[24] We call elements (sections of the text-morpheme or morpheme sequences) equivalent to each other if they occur in the environment of (other) identical or equivalent elements. And the first step in discourse analysis is to decide which elements are to be taken as equivalent to each other;[25] in other words, to situate verbal elements in a hierarchy of perspectives, forces, actions, words; to give them importance and significance because of their difference. The seven words "I murdered them because they were there" relate intentional forces and behavioural actions in a hierarchy, a perspective. The sentence not only states that a murder occurred but it is stated by the murderer as a confession, an act of admittance, and it invites exploration of motives and intentions with the relational word "because" and the confusing "they were there."

Performatives and Constatives

Speech act theorists make an important distinction between performatives and constatives in language acts which distinction impacts upon what I am writing here about intention formation and execution. Interpreted for my purposes here, a constative is a statement of an objective, external observable fact while a performative is the statement of an internal, observable fact. In other words, a sentence is a performative when it expresses a truth unique to the intentional structure of a particular individual. A sentence is a constative, (what I believe would be the traditional "declarative" sentence) when it expresses a truth that is

---

[23] Lenneberg, 589.

[24] Zelig Harris, "Discourse Analysis," in *The Structure of Language: Readings in the Philosophy of Language.* Edited by Jerry A. Fodor and Jerrold J. Katz, (New Jersey: Prentice-Hall, Inc., 1964), 359.

[25] Zelig Harris, 363-364.

observable to others as scientifically, objectively provable and true. With a performative, the truth is observable and scientifically provable only to the extent that it can be developed and explained by the individual " . . . by speaking, by pronouncing these words, I produce the (interior) *event* that they designate:"[26] Thus in place of the truth/falsity criterion, essential to constative, scientific language, speech act theorists substitute in the case of performative language the criterion of felicity and sincerity as opposed to infelicity and insincerity. The truth, the objectivity, of a performative rests with the sincerity and the felicity of the speaker to intend and mean what is said and to have the listener or reader understand that same intention and meaning. Others can only accept the truth of a performative, in the sense of a constative, a scientifically observable fact, if it is situated convincingly in a nexus of forces such that the speaker's sincerity and good will are not questioned and the statements about the person's interior life of intentional forces are accepted and recognised as scientifically, objectively true.

Speech act theory's illocutionary force activity is encompassed, deepened, and broadened with this concept of the performative. The "illocutionary act" is the speech performance examined in terms of the interior *context* of other forces and acts surrounding the locution, and also with reference to the concrete, conventional, discursive situation in which speech acquires, above and beyond its internal, personal meaning for the speaker (performative), a certain force of utterance in a community (constative). Speech act theorists distinguish between *meaning*, in the sense of performative, and *force*, in the sense of a single illocutionary act, to the extent that performative meaning is produced in the sequence of illocutionary acts or forces which series of forces constitute the performance of the meaning.

The statement of a meaningful fact about an individual's intentional structure is a performative constituted in a series of illocutionary forces and may be a scientifically agreed upon declaration, a constative, an objective truth. Cardinal Newman's assertion that he has a right to private judgement and decision with regard to his conversion (a performative) based upon an accumulation of

---

[26] Shosana Felman, *The Literary Speech Act: Don Juan with J.L. Austin, or Seduction in Two Languages*, translated by Catherine Porter, (Ithaca: Cornell University Press, 1983), 16.

probabilities and possibilities (various constatives and illocutionary forces) is an example of what I mean here.

The written text explaining intentional structure becomes an object, a phenomenon, a structure in itself, outside of consciousness, which the consciousness that constructed it then looks at as an object that may only capture an incidental, insignificant trace of the structure in consciousness.

Tennessee Williams writes importantly about language structures as illusions which communicate only traces in *The Glass Menagerie.* He creates the character of Tom who narrates his personal story about why he left home to join the Merchant Marine; but as Tom begins to narrate he says that he feels like he is looking through a transparent fourth wall into his home and his memory may be creating verbal illusions, performatives for him but non-constatives for others, because they are of things which really did not happen. They only happened to him. He makes the very telling point, it seems to me, that the magician gives the audience a behavioural illusion, a fantasy, an action that is a pretense, and makes it look completely convincing and real. The trick is an apparent constative, a declaration of fact, but has no illocutionary force, no constitutive base. He says that writers or narrators are like the magician in that they give the reader or listener some particular behavioural reality, some situation or story with settings and characters and plot development, in words, with words, but the verbal structure, the words, are only a trace, an illusion, an unreality, because they capture just one force in a sequence of forces and it is the sequence of forces which constitutes performatives.

> Tom: Yes, I have tricks in my pocket, I have things up my sleeve. But I am the opposite of a stage magician. He gives you illusion that has the appearance of truth. I give you truth in the pleasant guise of illusion.[27]

Vladimir Nabokov captures the sense of Williams' magician-writer analogy in this passage about his memory of his tutors:

---

[27] Tennessee Williams, *The Glass Menagerie*, (New York: A Signet Book of the New American Library, 1945), 27-29.

In thinking of my successive tutors, I am concerned less with the queer dissonances they introduced me to in my young life than with the essential stability and completeness of that life. I witness with pleasure the supreme achievement of memory, which is the masterly use it makes of innate harmonies and wandering tonalities of the past. I like to imagine, in consummation and resolution of those jangling chords something as enduring, in retrospect, as the long table on summer birthdays and namedays used to be laid for afternoon chocolate out of doors . . . . I see the tablecloth and the faces . . . . exaggerated, no doubt, by the same faculty of impassioned commemoration, of ceaseless return, that always makes me approach that table from the outside, . . . through a tremulous prism, I distinguish features, . . . I see . . . I note . . . . the pulsation of my thought mingles with that of the lead shadows and turns Ordo into Max and Max into Lenski and a Lenski into the schoolmaster, and the whole array of trembling transformations is repeated. And then, suddenly, . . . a torrent of sounds comes to life: enthusiastic hullabaloo, . . . like a background of wild applause.[28]

In this passage, Nabokov blends the sight of the table with the people and food and the sounds of the activity. Nabokov here portrays himself as sitting at his desk, remembering this scene and then writing it down. The illocutionary forces at the various Derridean centers of his consciousness are ones which try to remember and center this scene from childhood and his language captures some of the complexity of that act of remembering and centering and is then a performative. The text constitutes an internal reality as an objective fact.

Tennessee Williams and Vladimir Nabokov both look back and remember various crucial events in their lives and they then attempt to re-capture them from memory in writing. Their words express the interior, intentional activity of remembering and the words also capture the random, incoherent, fractured way that the memory works.

---

[28] Vladimir Nabokov, *Speak, Memory: An Autobiography Revisited*, (New York: G.P. Putnam's Sons, 194, 1948, 1949, 1950, 1960, 1966), 170-172.

70

Flannery O'Connor in Chapter Three of *The Violent Bear It Away* expresses in words the interior activity of the main character, Tarwater, when he comes to realise in a particular moment that he is being called to be a prophet and baptise his uncle's child.

The boy Tarwater had just experienced the death of his great uncle, with whom he had lived as father and son for many years, at breakfast one morning. He proceeds to go to the house of his uncle (the great uncle's son who had disowned his father because his father was raising Tarwater with religious beliefs) with a view to announcing the death and "doing what's needful." What, on the surface, appears to be a practical, straightforward matter is turned into an interior event in Tarwater where motivations, attitudes, desires and feelings congeal into the realisation that he has indeed been called to be a prophet and baptise his uncle's boy.

O'Connor first presents the boy Tarwater as deliberating painfully about announcing the death to the younger uncle. He is "scowling" and he is

> unpleasantly aware of the sky . . . as if he were alone in the presence of an immense eye . . . He had an intense desire to make himself known . . . and be congratulated for what he had done . . . He stared boldly hardening himself for the encounter. The quiet seemed palpable, waiting, demanding to be named and the sound of the knocker on the door "shattered" the silence as a noise, a racket, as energy filling his head. Tarwater continued to knock, echoing, kicking . . . until he stopped and the implacable silence descended again and filled him with a mysterious dread. (All quotations are taken from Chapter Three of the novel.)

This material is all in preparation for the interior activity that is about to occur, an activity that usually begins after a sudden shock, like finding someone dead or after moments of long, self-conscious silence. Tarwater is at first simply singlemindedly interested in communicating the fact that his great-uncle has just died (he's communicating this information to the uncle's son) but other interior, unexpected revelations will occur in the interchange.

The uncle himself, when he comes to understand that his father has died, is "intrigued by the symmetry and rightness . . . a perfect irony—he got what he deserved." Tarwater "expended all his energy announcing himself" and what he had done, such that he suddenly fell blank and stunned and remained stupidly silent. The "perceptible trace of scorn" which had earlier crossed his face was also gone. But when the uncle thought that this was "another one of his tricks," that the grandfather was not really dead, but was trying to find another sneaky way to baptise the boy, Tarwater "blanched" and "in his mind's eye, he saw the old man and . . . he stared shocked . . . at the uncle . . . he saw with terrible clarity that the great-uncle's death was a decoy to lead him [Tarwater] to do his 'unfinished business' and baptise the boy, Bishop."

Tarwater's perceptions may indeed be deranged and wrongheaded but my point is that O'Connor captures an interior process of intention formation in prose. Unlike Williams and Nabokov, O'Connor captures it as it is happening. Tarwater's face darkened and the expression hardened so that he could keep his thoughts, his newly discovered insights protected. The uncle has an entirely different agenda for the newly orphaned Tarwater. The reader gets less of the uncle's vision than Tarwater's, though. In fact, when Tarwater sees the boy Bishop standing in the background "then the revelation came, silent, implacable, direct as a bullet. He did not look into the eyes of any fiery beast nor did he see a burning bush. He only knew, with a certainty sunk in despair, that he was expected to baptise the child he saw and begin the life his great uncle had prepared for him."

O'Connor gives the reader that matrix of attitudes, ideas, beliefs, motivations which led Tarwater to form this intention but she does so using that stream of consciousness technique wherein the activity being portrayed is Tarwater's announcement of the death of the great uncle and the younger uncle deciding that he would now "make a man" of Tarwater. O'Connor gives Tarwater's thoughts and his futile attempts to shout "No!" The uncle attempted to "shake him (out of his reverie) slightly to penetrate his inattention" but Tarwater was by no means in any reverie of inattention. He was fixed on an interior activity which led to a decision, an intention, quite different from the uncle's and the uncle had no perception of what was occurring. The uncle just saw Tarwater as a new activity for himself, someone whom he could now mould and change. The uncle would correct all the mistakes made by his father and re-form the boy, Tarwater.

But, of course, Tarwater "heard nothing he [the uncle] said." He was just fixated on the child not five feet from him. He knew that the child recognised him, as John in Elizabeth's womb recognised Jesus in Mary's womb. The "old man himself had primed him from on high that he was the forced servant of God come to see that he was born again."

Tarwater yells "Git" at the boy and the child clambers up his father's leg which the father interprets as a natural rivalry between the boys, a newness, a strangeness between them, but O'Connor presents another level, another process in consciousness, in both the children, especially Tarwater who has now newly uncovered, discovered, his role as prophet, hitherto unrecognised.

Graham Greene's *Monsignor Quixote* also has a section that illustrates what I am saying about formation of intention. He has the Monsignor confect the Eucharist, the sacrament of the Body and Blood of the Lord, with words only, no bread or wine. In other words, the interior level of intention is an act, the utterance of the words another act and the bread and wine a third act. *Action*, reality, the presence of Jesus in this case, is effected at any of these levels and they each serve as constatives/performatives for the others.

The terms constative/performative of speech act theory are actually a reworking of the old Aristotelian-Thomistic "substance-accident" dichotomy. A substance is something constitutive, a constative, an essential, the essence of a thing while an accident is a performative, an incidental, a behavioural part of the thing but not its substance, its essence. The difference between substance/accident and constative/performative is that speech act theory suggests that something which appears to be an accidental may at another time be an essential, a substance, a constative, which is the root, source, and center of a particular nexus of other behaviours, performances and accidents.

Aristotelian-Thomistic categories allow for no such fluidity. The substance, the essence of a thing is always invisible, unreachable, singular while accidental manifestations abound but they are never substances.

In the last chapter of *Monsignor Quixote*, Graham Greene has the feeble monsignor attempt to celebrate a private Mass, but without any bread and wine. The monsignor had been given a sedative by the doctor to help him sleep but he still awoke at 1 a.m. not knowing where he was. He was given another sleeping pill and slept until 3 a.m. at which time he awoke and began to utter various non-sequiturs. Observers wondered whether he was truly delirious due to heavy sedation or dreaming some kind of dream.

When he leaves his bedroom to go to recite a private Mass, other characters follow him and he again appears to be delirious, stopping to speak to statues and utter more fragments.

He then proceeds rather rapidly through an "oddly truncated form" of the Mass, no epistle or gospel readings as if racing to the consecration, the point at which the bread and wine are changed into the body and blood of Jesus through the recitation of the last supper narrative.

The observers presume that he would wake up when he realises that there is no plate with bread on it and no cup but he didn't wake up; he proceeds through the rite "totally unaware that there was no bread or cup . . . he raised empty hands—the observers even knelt down out of 'custom' at the words of consecration. They thought he would wake up at communion when he finds nothing to eat or drink. They began to wonder if he would ever awaken from this sleepwalk. At communion, he takes the invisible bread from the invisible plate and lays nothing on his tongue. He does the same with the invisible cup but the observers saw the movement of his throat as he swallowed. As he distributes communion to the others, he dies.

In a conversation later in the book, the observers analyse the scene:

> "What we listened to last night could hardly be described as a Mass."
>
> "Are you sure of that?"
>
> "Of course I am. There was no consecration."
>
> "I repeat—are you sure?"
>
> "Of course I'm sure. There was no host and no wine."
>
> "Descartes, I think would have said rather more cautiously than you that he *saw* no bread or wine [and by extension, no body and blood of Christ is seen at a real Mass]."
>
> "You know as well as I do that there *was* no bread or wine."
>
> "I know as well as you—or as little—yes, I agree to that. But Msgr. Quixote quite obviously believed in the presence of bread and wine [and by extension many Christians, notab-

ly Catholics, obviously believe in the real presence of Christ]."

"Which of us is right?"

"We were."

"Very difficult to prove that logically, professor."

"You mean that I may have received communion?"

"You certainly did—in *his* mind. Does it matter to you?"

"To me, no. But I'm afraid in the eyes of your church I'm a very unworthy recipient. I am a Communist. One who has not been to confession for 30 years or more."

"Perhaps Msgr. Quixote knew your state of mind better than you do yourself. He encouraged you to take the host."

"There was no host . . . whatever Descartes may have said. You are arguing for the sake of arguing. You are misusing Descartes."

"Do you think that its more difficult to turn empty air into wine than wine into blood. Can our limited sense decide a thing like that. We are faced by an infinite mystery."

"I prefer to think that there was no host because I once did partly believe in a God and a little of that superstition remains. I'm afraid of mystery and too old to change. I prefer Marx to mystery."

The point that I wish to make by using these scenes from Graham Greene's *Monsignor Quixote*, in keeping with the tenets of speech act theory, is that transubstantiation, the Roman Catholic dogma which holds that the substance of the bread and wine, not the sensory accidentals of taste, touch, smell etc. are changed into the substance of the body and blood of Christ, not the accidents of his particular body and blood which can been seen, touch, tasted, smelled etc. is effected through the recitation of the words of the last supper narrative; Jesus' own words: "This is my body . . . this is my blood."

I wish to deflect the attention from the Aristotelian-Thomistic categories of substance and accident to the rhetorical theory of speech act which focuses on the substance (constatives) and accidents (performatives) of the words of the narrative. The words themselves are Aristotelian accidentals, particular forms in a particular language. In terms of speech act theory, they are locutionary acts-utterances. The Aristotelian-Thomistic essence or substance of the words, the utterances, the locutions is the illocutionary activity of intention, attitude and motivation formation in the utterer. The bread and wine are changed, transubstantiation occurs, through the utterance of the words which have their power, their authority, in the illocutionary structure, the substance, of Jesus as a person. Impossible as it is to do, Christians believe that the bread and wine change into the body and blood of Jesus simply because that is what he intended and so that is what is effected through the words. The power of the sacrament is in the utterance of the words of the narrative which are constituted in the illocutionary activity in the person of Jesus.

Speech act theory, explicated most fully in the work of John Searle and J.L. Austin, says that when words are uttered (and by extension when written) in a particular context, the words themselves become objects separate from the person who uttered or wrote them. The words become locutionary realities (accidentals, performatives) in themselves constituted in but separate from the illocutionary reality (the substance), the matrix of motivations, intentions, attitudes, and beliefs, of the person who uttered them. If the words themselves are considered as realities, acts, in themselves, constituted in the person, then they effect, they cause to happen what they say. Applied to the last supper narrative where the Eucharist was instituted, the anecdote from Graham Greene's *Monsignor Quixote* illustrates the theory.

When Jesus spoke the words at the last supper those many years ago, he was speaking from a particular point of view and his words, not only his words at the last supper but many of his words recorded in the gospels, especially his words which effected healing, are constituted in a matrix of illocutionary acts consisting of a variety of intentions, motivations, attitudes, feelings. This matrix can be called his consciousness—a compilation of the unconscious, subconscious, preconscious realms. Researchers, scripture scholars, archaeologists, paleontologists labor tirelessly to penetrate this matrix, this mystery. Speech act theory merely recognises the presence of this mystery within, this matrix of illocutionary acts in consciousness from which words are uttered. The words, the locutions, are a shadowy, veiled representation of the illocutionary matrix of motivations, intentions, attitudes, feelings which make up the consciousness of the person uttering them.

76

Traditional theology holds that the words together with the action, the bread and wine, confect the sacrament but I am saying that the words together with the illocutionary, interior action are what confect the sacrament. The word becomes the sacrament (or flesh) and hence no bread and wine are needed as illustrated with Monsignor Quixote. I intend to assert here that it is the utterance of the words of the narrative that effect a transubstantiation of the elements. It is the utterance of the words of the narrative which then becomes an invisible "thing," an object which has been breathed forth, that becomes the focus, the centre, and the bread and wine become the words and the words are rooted in the person of Jesus. When the bread is eaten, what is received are the words of Jesus which are constituted in the richer illocutionary matrix of his person. This is reminiscent of the earlier Hebrew prophet who was commanded by God to write down the words on the paper and then eat the paper and then he will have the word of God in him and will be able to speak that word, preach and prophesy.

> When I looked up there was a hand stretching out to me, holding a scroll. He unrolled it in front of me; it was written on front and back . . . . He then said, "Son of Man, eat what you see; eat this scroll, then go and speak to the House of Israel." I opened my mouth; he gave me the scroll to eat and then said, "Son of Man, feed on this scroll which I am giving to you and eat your fill." So I ate it, and it tasted sweet as honey. He then said, "Son of Man, go to the House of Israel and tell them what I have said."

> Ezekiel 2:9–3:4

Referentiality

I would like to conclude this chapter with a discussion of referentiality, especially in light of examples like Nabokov's reference to his tutors, and Williams' representation of Tom referring to an event, and my earlier example of murder with no apparent motive and O'Connor's representation of Tarwater's consciousness and Greene's Monsignor Quixote.

Language, through linguistic structuring, *refers* to forces and complexes of forces in the intentional structures just as it has the rhetorical potential to refer to external events and behaviours. The complex of forces is the constative and the language expressing those forces is the performative; the language gives external validity and reliability to the internal. The language 'performance' is 'constituted' in the interior matrix of forces. External, observable events and behaviours are performatives in the sense that they can be observed by a number of people, as opposed to interior life which can only be observed and experienced by the individual. The external, observable behaviour is the performative, like the complex of illocutionary forces, and the language which summarises and expresses that behaviour is a constative; the language gives the performative behaviour an external validity and reliability, a proof of existence so to speak. Language has this ability to refer to and constitute and the more closely and carefully it succeeds in referring, the more fine-grained it is. An external behaviour consists of a series of external events which comprise the particular behaviour and make it a unit. An internal behaviour similarly consists of a series of internal acts (forces, neurochemical transmissions) which comprise the activity. When a sentence communicates one of these behaviours or a part of one of them, the sentence is a performative to the extent that it is "performing" the action already performed. The interior word is the force which constitutes the behaviour.

Eugene Ionesco executes a wonderful verbal spoof on referentiality with his "Bobby Watson" sequence in *The Bald Soprano* in which every person in a particular family, the Watsons, with whom the Smiths are friends, is named Bobby, such that by merely naming them, true reference is lost. Ionesco has the Smiths come to distinguish the Watsons by blood relation, grandmother, cousin, aunt, sister, and then some distinctive behaviour which separates them but the use of the language term, "Bobby Watson," as a referent becomes useless.[29] Abbott and Costello's famous "Who's" on First, "What's" on Second and "I don't Know's" on Third is a comic example of referentiality problems.

---

[29] Eugene Ionesco, *Four Plays: The Bald Soprano, The Lesson, Jack, or The Submission, The Chairs*, translated by Donald M. Allen, (New York: The Grove Press, Inc., 1958), pp. 12 ff.

78

John Searle discusses referentiality as the relation between expressions as definite descriptions and proper names.[30] The difference for Searle is in his distinction between what he calls "the direction of fit"[31] between words and the world. I think that his "direction of fit" is comparable to the classical concept of appropriateness or decorousness with regard to rhetorical expression and also parallels such theories as Grice's co-operative principle. There is a complementarity between the words uttered by the speaker and the way things are in the world of other speakers. Speech act theorists like Searle focus on the illocutionary points being directed to other speakers in a "fit" sort of way dependent upon the psychological sincerity and good will of the speaker.

Searle distinguishes between the referential and the attributive use of words: attributive use is a group of words which refer to "whoever it was who murdered Smith," whereas referential use is that group of words which points to the real person, the singular individual, who actually did murder Smith. Reference, Searle writes, is achieved by a variety of syntactical devices (proper names, definite descriptions, pronouns, demonstratives) and is determined by the relation between the speaker and object referred to.[32] Therefore, referentiality can contain definite descriptions which refer literally and directly to a particular object but they can also contain words which, by implication, suggest other objects indirectly, attributively, pointed to by the words.

This referential-attributive distinction is closely related to the *de re–de dicto* as well as constative-performative distinction.[33] The *de re–de dicto* distinction is in short a distinction between ways of reporting beliefs. In a *de dicto* report, the entire content of the report is internal, intentional, that is a constative, an attributive reference in the sense that an object cannot be pointed to because the "object" is in the mind of the speaker. While in a *de re* report, on the other hand, the entire content of the report is external, objective, that is a per-

---

[30] John Searle, *Expression and Meaning: Studies in the Theory of Speech Acts*, (Cambridge University Press, 1979), xi.

[31] Searle, *Expression and Meaning*, 3.

[32] Searle, *Expression and Meaning*, 142.

[33] Searle, *Expression and Meaning*, 157.

formative, a referential series of words which has an object that can be pointed to and is scientifically, objectively provable and observable as an object in time and space.[34] Graphically:

de re	de dicto
an objective "thing" (res)	a "spoken" thing (dico)
a performance (ative)	a constative
—declared, external	—a declared, internal
a reference outside	attributive
—points to real, physical object	—points to internal, non—physical object

Searle's point is just that linguistics concerns itself with the empirical, observable facts about natural human languages; the *de re* performatives point to real references; the *de dicto* constatives cannot be pointed to directly (attributive).[35]

One of the purposes of language is communication. One of the goals of rhetoric and linguistics is clarity and fineness in communication. Speech act theorists have reduced language to a unit of the type called "illocutionary." The problem, as elaborated by Searle, (at least an important problem) for language philosophy and theory is to describe how we get from the sounds of the voice or markings on the paper back to these irreducible units called illocutionary acts. And I have argued that we get from sounds to illocutionary acts by studying the sounds, or the groupings of marks on paper, in terms of their relation to each other, and this relation refers both really (*de re*, performative) and attributively (*de dicto*, constative) to the series of illocutionary acts, a complex of forces, constatives which I am calling the intentional structures. An internal, illocutionary act (performative) can also be constituted in another illocutionary force which becomes the previous illocutionary act's constative. A performative may be a grouping of illocutionary acts in an intentional nexus of constitutive forces. This is then paralleled in performative grouping of external words and behaviours constituted in a range of interior acts and forces.

---

[34] Searle, *Expression and Meaning*, 158-159.

[35] Searle, *Expression and Meaning*, 162.

Each of these articulated by Searle (these forces, acts, attributes, references) is an element in a *context*, and it is by virtue of referential-transitional elements between their elements and particular things in the world that contexts are anchored to the things and situations which they are about. Singular terms, sounds or markings, refer to things as objects (internal forces, acts, performatives or external events, persons, situations) and the terms establish among themselves referential–attributive connections through syntactical–grammatical links in a referential chain.[36] It is my point, after Chastain, that in many contexts, referential linkage can only be established and explained attributively by speaker's intentions.[37] Single sentences, as referential-attributive propositions, are as a nest of possibilities.[38] "I murdered them because they were there" is a single sentence in which an author like Truman Capote in *In Cold Blood* sees the "nest of possibilities" for an exposition of a referential, *de re*, event of a murder with no apparent motive at the same time that it is a "nest of possibilities" for an exposition of an attributive, *de dicto*, constative/performative event of the intentional structure of the murderer.

My aim in this chapter has been to elaborate the ways in which the tools of rhetoric, language philosophy and linguistics can be used to represent interior, intentional structures in constitutive as well as performative ways. I shall now proceed to Thomas DeQuincey's, Geoffrey Chaucer's, Graham Greene's and Henry Fielding's verbal structures (their rhetoric, language and linguistics) through which they elaborate activities, behaviours and intentional states.

> *Telemachus: Mother, why do you grudge our own dear*
> *minstrel the joy of song, wherever his thought may lead? . . .*
> *Men like best a song that rings like morning in their ears.*
>
> Homer, *The Odyssey*
> Book I, ll. 210–211, 215–216

---

[36] Charles Chastain, "Reference and Context," in *Minnesota Studies in the Philosophy of Science*, Volume VII, *Language, Mind, and Knowledge*, edited by Keith Gunderson, (Minneapolis: The University of Minnesota Press, 1975), 211-214.

[37] Chastain, 221.

[38] Chastain, 227.

CHAPTER FOUR

From Literature

"Eek Plato seith, whoso kan hym rede,
The wordes moote be cosyn to the dede. "

Geoffrey Chaucer, *Canterbury Tales*,
"General Prologue," lines 741-2

I wish now to look more closely at specific examples of verbal structures, prose narratives, which exemplify the mediations of the intentional, verbal, and behavioural structures. These cases in point will be Thomas DeQuincey's narration of the morning that he left Manchester as written in his autobiography, *The Confessions of an English Opium Eater*, Geoffrey Chaucer's narration of the story of *Troilus and Criseyde*, Graham Greene's *The End of the Affair* which details the beginnings of the adulterous affair, and Henry Fielding's story of "The Unfortunate Gilt" in *Joseph Andrews*. In focusing on these verbal structures, the language, the rhetoric, of these narrations, I am making them the central and primary worlds, but only to the extent that their surface structures communicate the intentional structures of the characters whom the authors have created. The focus switches to the behaviour, in DeQuincey's case, when he leaves Manchester at a specific point in time. The focus switches to the intentional structure when DeQuincey deliberates in retrospect about the rightness of that decision. Chaucer and Greene focus on the behaviours of couples, Troilus and Criseyde and Sarah and Maurice: how they meet and fall in love and the consequences. Henry Fielding does the same in a section of *Joseph Andrews*.

The authors change the focus when they articulate the intentional-motivational structures of their characters which structures constitute their behaviours.

Each of these stories has a traditional plot structure, a narrative sequence of behaviours and events, but each of them also has an insightful articulation of the intentional states of the characters. As I have indicated in the previous chapters, the activities of the plot parallel the activities of the characters' intentional states and each can be arranged in various perspectives and gestalts.

Troilus and Criseyde

Chaucer's poem is a verbal structure, a piece of Middle English literature, which communicates both an intentional-motivational structure and a behavioural one. He creates this fiction, this sequence of behavioural events, of the ill-fated love of the fictional characters Troilus and Criseyde and sets the scene for the tragic turn in that relationship with Criseyde's apparent infidelity when, early in the poem, Chaucer carefully delineates the development of their relationship from its beginning with a special focus on their interior, intentional lives.

Troilus' "double sorwe,"[1] that is, his going from being in "wo" to being "wele" and then back to "wo again" has to do with his ability or inability to form an intention to be faithful to Criseyde with whom he had apparently fallen in love at first sight. Criseyde, in her turn, is later accused of infidelity and Chaucer also carefully traces the formation of her intention to be faithful to Troilus. A careful consideration of Books One and Two of the poem illustrates how Chaucer's verbal structure, his rhetoric, his careful description, communicates the formation of Troilus' and Criseyde's feelings about each other and their intentions to be faithful.

Troilus' *behavioural* condition of being in sorrow and depressed stems from his *intentional state*. Criseyde's *behavioural* condition of being "unfaith-

---

[1] Geoffrey Chaucer, "Troilus and Criseyde," in *The Complete Poetry and Prose of Geoffrey Chaucer*, edited by John H. Fisher, (New York: Holt, Rinehart and Winston), p. 403, line 1.

ful" stems also from her *intentional state* and the behaviours are explained, complemented, supplemented by an articulation of the intentions.

Troilus is introduced guiding his fellow knights through a crowded street. As with most any person, whether real or fictional, we usually meet them *in medias res*; that is, he has developed a certain way of approaching life based upon his experiences and he has also formulated some pattern of intention formation, organisation of his illocutionary forces, his motivations; therefore, we also meet them *in medias dicta*; that is, he has developed a certain way of thinking, feeling and speaking based upon the way he accumulates and arranges his forces within.

In Troilus' case, Chaucer tells us that he is scornful of love, suggesting that he may have had some unsuccessful experience in a love relationship, causing him to be scornful (Bk. I, l. 303), although there could be any number of intentional states to explain the scornful disposition. He watches his fellow knights react to the beautiful women in the crowd and he makes fun of their sighing and pining over these women. He sets himself above this silly, adolescent infatuation. He warns his fellow knights that love is foolish and uncertain. Troilus will not allow himself to be attracted by these women until his eyes fall "by chance" on Criseyde and he is astonished at her beauty and at his own unusual reaction to her, since he has apparently worked very hard to steel himself so carefully against this kind of reaction; so he decides to look more closely at her to see exactly what it is about her that is getting this reaction out of him.

> *And sodeynly he wax therwith astoned,*
> *An gan hire bet biholde yn thrifty wyse.*
> *"O mercy God," thoughte he, "wher hastow woned,*
> *That art so fair and goodly to devyse?"*
> *Therwith his herte gan to sprede and ryse,*
> *And softe sighed lest men myghte hym here,*
> *And caught ayen his firste pleyinge chere.*

Book I, ll. 275 ff.

Here then are the initial conditions for Troilus' formation of any intention to involve himself in a permanent love relationship with Criseyde. The fact that he "fell in love with her at first sight" is a primary force in the formation of his intention and the fact that he had steeled himself against such natural feelings is a second force which relates to this sudden fall. For all intents and purpose, he experiences that natural reaction that people often feel towards each other but then misinterprets the reaction as "true love" and proceeds to intend a lifelong fidelity.

He presumes that there must be something special about her for him to feel this, and so he wants to investigate more closely rather than realise that he has steeled himself for so long against these natural feelings that when he does feel them, he attaches undue importance to the person for whom he feels them. He might have examined more closely the fact that he was having these feelings and not been so surprised by them; rather than focus on Criseyde as some "one and only" special person whom he must love always and ever.

The formation of the intention to love Criseyde for the rest of his life begins at this key juncture and revolves around these two interior forces of having decided not to love again and then falling in love at this behavioural event of seeing Criseyde.

All of Criseyde's "parts" create a perfect woman for Troilus and her movements evidence honour, estate and nobility. She smiled back at him and he was in awe and "wonder" at her movements and face. Her smile quickened his desire and affection. Her vision fixed itself deeply in his mind and he had to maintain his scornful exterior for his fellow knights while he "sighed deeply" inside. He felt himself die in her look. He could not get her or her look out of his mind; she had "shot through" him. And here Chaucer describes, in a series of what I call secondary interior forces, vividly and clearly the experience of infatuation that may be a prelude to the formation of the intention to love and be faithful to someone for a longer period of time.

This initial experience is crucial in Troilus' formation of his intention to love and remain faithful to Criseyde for the rest of his life. The primary behavioural event of falling in love at first sight is followed by a primary intentional decision to investigate her more closely. This is followed by an elaboration of a series of secondary, interior forces which become performatives, explaining his infatuation that has been established.

Chaucer has the narrator pause to reflect for a moment on why and how Troilus could possibly have considered himself above this common human experience of sexual attraction and fascination. Human beings experience these feelings for each other as part of their human nature; why did Troilus feel that he was exempt or that he could force himself to be exempt? He scorned love and now it had turned round and enslaved him. "The strongest, the wittiest, the greatest" have all been overcome by love. Love, or more likely, infatuation, was what brought great woe as well as great comfort and ease. Both love and infatuation have in their own ways appeased the cruellest heart and both can bring degrees of suffering. Chaucer suggests through his narrator that this experience is a way for Troilus to re-touch his own humanness with which he had lost touch, and if Troilus had realised this he may not have formed the intention to pursue Criseyde.

Troilus goes home, sits and sighs, thinks and dreams about her. He considers this a "right good adventure" and he decides that he will keep his feeling secret for awhile and determine a way that he can get her to notice him and of course, get her to respond to him and feel the same way about him. Troilus prays to God that he might win Criseyde. His infatuation causes him to become melancholic, which his friends start to notice and wonder about. He looks pale and in ill-health. He feels like he is being tossed about by contrary winds. He wonders why he feels so badly if love is supposed to be so good. Secondary intentional forces begin to accumulate, connect and become part of the interior gestalt or performative which might be called "infatuation."

His subsequent attempts to get Criseyde to notice him are unsuccessful and this makes him more and more sad and frustrated at the same time that it causes him to burn with greater love. He wishes to die so that this languishing and yearning for an object he cannot seem to attain will end. His obsession with her and his desire to die indicate an unsteady interior disposition upon which he bases the formation of his intention to love, permanence and fidelity.

Another individual in a similar position might give up the fight. If he has exhausted all possible means of communicating with her, then obviously, a relationship involving love, permanence and fidelity is not part of his fate. The obsession, languishing and mourning, are interior qualities affecting his ability to form an intention of permanence and fidelity. Troilus' intention to love and remain faithful to Criseyde turns obsessive and is done to appease his own emotional pain rather than out of true love for her.

His friend Pandarus, also Criseyde's uncle, recognising the situation, intercedes to help and direct. This is a major intercession, a primary activity in the plot development and becomes a primary element in Troilus' formation of intention to pursue Criseyde. Pandarus' advice and intercession become a new "input" into Troilus' compilation of intentional forces.

In effect, Pandarus suggests that Troilus make his feelings and intentions known to Criseyde which action would be a major behavioural advance in his favour. Pandarus points out that anything is better than this obsessive languishing and mourning. The least he could do is let her know how he feels and if she rejects him and he kills himself, then at least he is doing so for a noble, honourable cause and has pursued her as far as possible. But he is apparently so shy and afraid of rejection that he puts it all in the hands of Pandarus, who agrees to speak to Criseyde for him. This action becomes a secondary behavioural step. Having this "middleman" further complicates the situation because only Troilus can and should express these feelings; to communicate them through someone else muddles them. It would have been better had Pandarus encouraged Troilus to speak to Criseyde himself; Troilus could have used Pandarus as a testing ground to practice articulating his feelings.

Pandarus' visit with Criseyde is, as expected, overlaid with manipulation, and when this occurs the formation of a clear, honest intention on her part is considerably restricted. Pandarus begins by innocently praising this warrior Troilus and then casually talking about his avuncular concern and respect for her. He encourages her to be open to new adventures and hopes that she is looking for new experiences which would be profitable to her. A primary element which becomes a primary force in the nexus of forces in Criseyde's intentional structure is this invitation to openness to new experiences and the profession of love and concern of her uncle for her well-being.

Chaucer then gives a first insight into Criseyde's consciousness by telling us that she is aware that there is something strange about her uncle's solicitations; she is aware that he seems to have some ulterior motive. These secondary interior forces are added to the nexus of the care of the uncle and the advice that she be open to adventure.

Criseyde is presented as a woman who has some sense of herself, who she is, and what her desires and interests are. She responds to events in her life quite naturally, as they occur, according to her best instincts and desires, in a true Derridean, non-violent attitude and in this case she is suspicious of her uncle Pandarus' motives, who, it seems, is responding according to the Husserlean motivation to structure and bracket. She embodies, according to my earlier analysis, the Derridean natural attitude which does not want to do violence to the natural course of interior and exterior events and forces. Pandarus is more in keeping with Husserl's natural standpoint which wants to bracket and structure and execute in a particular way, excluding some forces and circumstances in favour of others.

Arthur Mizener analyses Criseyde sympathetically by arguing that *she* is a central, significant, primary event in Troilus' life but he is not such an important event in her life.[2] Mizener argues that Criseyde acts throughout the story in keeping with her own natural, non-violent, non-manipulative attitude. She is an "event," a bracket, in this story of Troilus' "double sorwe" in congruence with other events for him. Her "infidelity" with Diomede in the Greek camp is seen by Mizener as a quite natural one. Just as Troilus' response to her is a quite natural one, her initial, natural response to him is not one of a natural attraction and interest, except through the manipulation of her uncle. This is an important, significant beginning to her relationship with Troilus and her process of forming any intentions about him.

Pandarus, by line 320 of Book II, has made the full revelation of Troilus' love for her and *he* begins to cry. He advises her to return the love and she begins to cry. She feels as if she is "constraining" her heart (a violence) to do something (bracket, structure, direct) that she really does not want to do, should not do. At this crucial point, she agrees that it might be better if Troilus "got over her." In time, his strong feelings would abate. But Pandarus is the one who feels that they are made for each other and he says that he will return and die with Troilus if she refuses. A primary, significant force in Criseyde's ability or inability to form an intention to love Troilus is this initial reaction that maybe he should "just get over her."

She is left to herself to think about this and Chaucer allows readers into her thoughts as he allowed them into Troilus' thoughts. As much as she feels

---

[2] Arthur Mizener, "Character and Action in the Case of Criseyde, " *PMLA*, LIV, (1939), 65.

that this is probably not a good thing to pursue and respond to, she is also enticed and fascinated by the idea of a new adventure (a key element in the forces in her consciousness) and the obviously attractive idea of having someone else so devoted, infatuated and interested in her. Her response revolves around the impulse "to have an adventure." There is no love commitment, nor is there any promise of fidelity or permanence. A primary force in the formation of her intention to involve herself with Troilus is her interest in having an adventure for herself. She has not even seen him yet.

Donald Howard analyses lines 596-931 of Book II as key lines in the formation of Criseyde's intentions and attitudes regarding Troilus.[3] Chaucer's expertise as a writer focuses on his ability to write an interior monologue which captures the associative, abstract thought of Criseyde. These are secondary forces in Criseyde's interior state which are added to the desire to have an adventure. Howard says that this is the "miracle" of Chaucer's art and it is the miracle of language that it is capable of allowing consciousness, intentional structures, to be articulated like this for others. Howard focuses on Chaucer's replication of Criseyde's fluctuation between fear and fascination, reticence and attraction, insecurity and independence, emotion and reason. Different stimuli trigger different ranges of force and response in her which are the key elements in the formation of her intention to speak and act in particular ways.

Howard points out the affinity between the chance associations in Criseyde's mind and the Boethian philosophy of free will which says that God can see these free choices and associations but does not cause them. All of Criseyde's reasonings and vacillations, her stream of inner associations and conversation with herself, climax in her dream about the white eagle tearing out her heart. Howard maintains that the validity of her decision in favour of Troilus resides in this unconscious dream sequence which indicates that she actually feels that her heart is being torn out in this forced association with Troilus. When she finally does see Troilus for the first time, regaled in all of his knightly honor and military glory and prowess, she feels "drunk," as if someone "yaf me

---

[3] Donald Howard, "Experience, Language and Consciousness: *Troilus and Criseyde*, II, 596-931," in *Medieval Literature and Folklore Studies: Essays in Honor of Franicis Lee Utley*, (edited by Jerome Mandel and Bruce A Rosenberg, New Brunswick, New Jersey: Rutgers University Press, 1970), 173.

drynke" and Karla Taylor connects this with the "love-potion"[4] tradition of Tristan and Isolde. Troilus is fresh, young and vigorous and Criseyde allows his appearance to sink softly into her heart, which causes the feeling of elation, intoxication. Donald Howard concludes sympathetically in Criseyde's favour that she is a woman controlled by an onslaught of unconscious, unintended, unformed forces and associations as well as the same natural impulses of infatuation and sexual attraction that Troilus has. True freedom, Howard says, is the awareness of these interior forces, not so much as fated or providential, but as forces which can be doubted, denied, changed or ignored; forces which can be incorporated and formed into an intentional structure and stance or not. The choice may be to be indifferent to fate, chance and the material, transitory world which "passeth soone as floures faire."

There are five major forces at work in Criseyde's formation of an intention to pursue a relationship with Troilus which are articulated as performatives in Chaucer's text:

1. her initial impulse to forget the whole thing;

2. her fascination with the idea of a new adventure with someone, a famous soldier, who is so taken with her and will die if she does not have pity on him;

3. her dream (an unconscious or subconscious force) of the white eagle taking her heart out;

4. her allowing herself then to see him and feel the effects, the magnetism, of his physical attractiveness *and* her power over him, giving him a chance.

5. her fear of the gossip of other people who will accuse her of falling in love at first sight.

In fact, Criseyde may have fallen unconsciously in love with the idea that she had power over the life of someone so powerful, a warrior, one who took others' lives. And it is this "power business" that comes to be another important

---

[4] Karla Taylor, "A Text and Its Afterlife: Dante and Chaucer," *Comparative Literature*, Winter, 1983, 35 (1) 1.

force in Criseyde's formation of an intention to be faithful to Troilus. She has made no advertence to any notion of faithfulness, permanence or love. She is apparently responding in order to be helpful and have an adventure, a little fun and some power over a man who is powerful; probably a somewhat natural, spontaneous reaction. As she looks at Troilus and considers the circumstances, she feels that she "might" be "inclined" to love him. She could talk herself into fidelity, permanence and love.

In the course of the lines following 697, she vacillates again:

> *now was hire herte warm, now was it colde . . . . Al were it nat to done to graunte hym love, yet for his worthynesse it were honeste with swych a lord to dele, for myne estat, and also for his hele . . . . Ek sith I wot for me is his distresse, I ne oughte nat for that thyng hym despise, sith it is so he meneth in good wyse. . . . Ne avounter, certeyn, seyth men, is he non . . . . Men myghten demen that he loveth me. What dishonour were it unto me, this? . . . and yet his lif al lyth now in my cure. But swych is love, and ek myn aventure.*

Book II, ll. 697 ff

At the beginning of Book III, Criseyde wants to know Troilus' "intentions" from Pandarus, who tells her that Troilus wishes to love and serve her in all humility and truth (ll. 131 ff.). Criseyde then agrees to a relationship with him, but cautions him that he will not have complete "soveraynete (l. 171)" over her. This offer to love him as a sister is not accepted and she does not want him to kill himself so she will allow him to love and serve her. But she still has complete "soveraynete" over him because she is doing the allowing.

Suddenly, in the midst of these ruminations, she becomes overcome with a moment of fear—as if overshadowed by some cloud—a fear that almost made her fall down. She interprets this experience of fear, and interprets it rightfully, it seems to me, as a fear of losing her own security and freedom. Why should she put herself under the constraints of love, she asks. She says that she knows that love is stormy and men stop loving women and the woman is left to weep in pain. She is afraid of everybody gossiping about her with these sudden stops and starts of love. But she is attracted by Pandarus' suggestion that she be open to new adventures and experiences even if they fail. But again, in the course of these deliberations, she says that she feels her heart quake with a dread and fear, a loss of hope, as it were, so she goes into the garden to pace up and down, think and relax. And, according to my thesis in this book about the formation of intention and the functional importance of language in that formation, this quickening of the heart and the feeling of loss of hope are internal indicators of an unpreparedness and a unreadiness to make any decision but are indicative that a preparatory formation is occurring and needs to be examined. They are secondary forces in Criseyde's interior state and are described by Chaucer in this sequence in the garden. Her recognition that she has power over Troilus and he does *not* have power over her is a primary force in her intention to go ahead with the relationship.

Another significant moment, an imaginative moment which parallels the dream of the eagle in Criseyde's formation of her intentions and feelings about Troilus, occurs in this walk in the garden when she hears Antigone singing a song about love (p. 436, ll. 814 ff.). Antigone, in her song, assumes the persona of a young girl who is in love and promises to be humble and "true to her intention," to give as best she can and to give in security and without fear. At this point in time, Criseyde intends basically to try it out and see what happens. Her experiences of fear indicate that something is amiss with her involvement and the young lover in Antigone's song prays for fidelity—to serve attentively, well, unwearied and true. The singer is thankful to God that she can experience love like this in her heart, the kind of love and faithfulness that Criseyde is not experiencing. The singer in the poem intends to lead a virtuous life, avoiding any manner of sin and the song concludes on a note of sadness for those who are too wicked or envious to love or just incapable of love and so defame it because they don't know it. This poem (within the poem) becomes as manipulative an influence on Criseyde as is Pandarus. It is an exterior input in the form of a verbal structure which triggers internal indicators in Criseyde. We are told that Criseyde was married once and there is no reason to assume that there was no love in her marriage and that she is not called to love again; there is no reason to presume that she has had similar experiences to Troilus and may have steeled herself against love. The brightness, radiance and achievement of true love is worth the sorrow and pain needed to accomplish it. Criseyde at this point seems uninterested in any sorrow, pain or gossip in her life and is even less interested in committing to marriage again.

Chaucer has Criseyde go to bed with all of this in her heart and fall a-sleep "to the love song of a nightingale." And it is during this sleep that she has the dream of the white eagle snatching her heart out. The dream suggests that she is being "forced" into this relationship with Troilus.

The next significant piece of external, behavioural input for Criseyde is the letter she receives from Troilus via Pandarus. She does not like the idea of having anything put into writing and again questions her uncle's involvement in this whole affair. She is annoyed with the uncle because he insists that she answer the letter and do things his way. She does not intend any permanence or fidelity with Troilus and she does not want to be forced to write things that she does not mean.

She re-reads his letter privately and feels that it is quite appropriate and pleasant but she does not know what to answer. Pandarus tells her just to write and thank him for the letter and wish him well. She does so but she feels like a sister and tells Pandarus that this is painful for her. She wants Troilus to live and be happy but she doesn't want to promise anything she can't deliver. She clearly wants to love Troilus "from afar, like a sister." Troilus is even more distressed when he hears about this sister-love from Pandarus who tells him that he will arrange to have Criseyde in a position where she will be forced to love him at which point any legitimate formation of a true intention is of course annulled.

Richard Osberg locates the "essential" Criseyde in the lines in Book Five where she is described as: "Charitable, estatlich, lusty, and fre; Ne nevere mo lakked hire pite; Tendre-hearted, slydynge in corage."[5]

In effect, her intentional structure at this time is unable or unwilling to be constant, committed, faithful. Her interior dispositions and sentiments, the formation of any number of forces into intentions, will depend upon events with which she will "slyde," as Chaucer writes. She can only assure Troilus that she will sincerely try to return from Greece where she has been sent as part of a

---

[5] Richard Osberg, "Between Motion and Action: Intentions and Ends in Chaucer's *Troilus*," *Journal of English Literary History*, Summer 48 (2), 257.

governmental trade. The fact that she "slides with events" is a significant, Derridean-like component of Criseyde's consciousness and her ability to form any permanent love relationship.

When she arrives in Greece and meets Diomede and tells him that she loved her dead husband and makes no reference to Troilus, the logical conclusion is that she is lying and being unfaithful because she does not mention Troilus. But when her words are examined in the light of what Richard Osberg and the lines in Book Five say are essential to her character, that is, that her courage slides with the circumstances, then it is quite understandable that she would respond freely to Diomede. She made no promises to Troilus; she assured him that she would do her best to return but the circumstances dictated that she not return.

The words that Criseyde speaks are true, honest and sincere because they come from her heart, her beliefs, which are, to be sure, inconstant, as are her actions. Eugene Vance applies the tenets of speech act theory to Criseyde's behaviour. According to speech act theory, which I discussed earlier, the words, the verbal structures, are just as much an act, a performance, as are the particular behaviours themselves that may or may not accompany them. When Criseyde says that she will do her best to return, she in effect means just that. She is not promising that she will return; she says that she will "do her best" to return. When Diomede asks her if she has ever loved and she tells him that she loved her dead husband, this is indeed true; she articulates with her words a past act. She does not love Troilus; she feels sorry for him.

Eugene Vance considers the entire poem of *Troilus and Criseyde* to be an extended series of illocutionary speech acts of Troilus, Criseyde and Pandarus in the form of interior monologues and dialogues.[6] Criseyde's intention to love and be faithful to Troilus is seriously complicated and distorted by Pandarus' involvement. The complexity and confusion of forces in Criseyde necessarily issue in a complex and confused series of words and behaviours. The singleminded thrust of forces in Troilus issue in a singleminded effort to win Criseyde. Troilus brackets and structures all of the incoming perceptions and feelings into

---

[6] Eugene Vance, "'Mervelous Signals': Poetics, Sign Theory, and Politics in Chaucer's *Troilus*," *New Literary History* X (1979), 239.

a system with which he feels comfortable whereas Criseyde does no such bracketing and systematising.

Troilus and Pandarus are the Husserlean phenomenologists who bracket
interior forces into intentional structures from which they will behave while
Criseyde is the Derridean metaphysician who allows her interior forces to
proceed ('slide') as they do, quite naturally, with very little bracketing and
structuring, committing and promising. When she is forced to bracket, systematise, make decisions and form intentions, she slides and recoils.

Vance contends that Chaucer evidences the acute awareness that speech,
verbal structures, are kinds of behaviour by which social action is achieved. In
the Prologue to the *Canterbury Tales* Chaucer quotes Plato's dialogue the
Phaedrus: "the word is cousin to the deed."[7] Speech and behaviour relate to
each other to the extent that they come from the same source, the illocutionary
forces in the heart and mind, the consciousness, the intentional structure of the
particular person performing the behaviour or uttering the word. Chaucer
focuses on Troilus and Criseyde's words as speech acts which are both performatives and constatives. Statements which assert realities that find their substance in the illocutionary activity, the association of forces, of the person (in
other words only the person could utter this particular truth) can be both constative and performative.

The concepts of the constative and performative which I developed in
Chapter Three apply here to Troilus and Criseyde. Troilus' and Criseyde's
words and behaviours are "performatives" in the sense that they are constituted
in the interior truths and forces, intentions and motivations. They are constatives
in the sense that they constitute the forces, motives and intentions. If the word
or behaviour returns to the person and directs the person's interior motivations
and intentions, then that word is a constative; it constitutes the person's interior
life. In contrast, if a word or behaviour returns to a person and simply mirrors
the random motivations and intentions there, those words or behaviours function
as performatives, that is, they "perform" what is actually happening.

---

[7] Geoffrey Chaucer, "The Prologue" to the *Canterbury Tales*, in *The Complete Prose and
Poetry of Geoffrey Chaucer*, edited by John H. Fisher, (New York: Holt, Rinehart and
Winston,) p. 22, line 742.

Ellen Schauber and Ellen Spolsky also refer to speech act theory in relation to Chaucer's "pardoner" and by extension, in relation to his Criseyde.[8] In order for any promises to be made and kept in the external, behavioural forum, certain pre-conditions need to exist which Criseyde obviously did not have. She is not able to perform a promise of fidelity because she does not intend it and Chaucer elaborates very carefully the process of her inability to form such an intention. He offers a series of major and minor incidents which I have called illocutionary forces in the intentional structures, words and actions in the behavioural structures, and words in the verbal, explanatory structure. Words and deeds are "cousins" to thoughts and feelings. Chaucer's words in his stories are "cousins" to his own thoughts about fidelity and commitment but he encourages his readers to take whatever lesson they wish from their reading. Readers' acts of reading likewise cause thoughts and feelings to arise and issue in words and deeds for readers.

Leonora and Bellarmine

I would like to contrast Chaucer's Troilus, Criseyde and Diomede with Henry Fielding's Leonora, Horatio and Bellarmine from *Joseph Andrews*. The story is contained in Chapters 4 and 6 of Book Two of the novel and is entitled "The History of Leonora, or the Unfortunate Jilt." After a brief summary, I will look closely at Fielding's language, the rhetoric of intention-motivation formation.

The poor Horatio falls in love with Leonora and asks her to marry him. They become engaged. She meets the rich, sophisticated Bellarmine and "falls" in love with him. She is confused about what to do about Horatio. Her aunt, aware that Bellarmine is rich and would bring money into the family, advises her to go with Bellarmine. The aunt volunteers to inform Horatio of this change but Horatio arrives unexpectedly on Leonora and Bellarmine together and discovers Leonora's changed affections. He seriously wounds Bellarmine in a duel and Leonora devotes herself to nursing Bellarmine back to health. When he

---

[8] Ellen Schauber and Ellen Spolsky, "Conversational Noncooperation: The Case of Chaucer's Pardoner," *Language and Style*, 16, 1983, 249.

returns to health, he visits Leonora's father to "ask for her hand," but actually to ask for her dowry, which the father does not have. Leonora will get her share of his money when he dies, not when she marries. Bellarmine decides against marrying her, returns to France and writes her a letter, suggesting that her father would not allow her to marry. Leonora, now the subject of conversation and ridicule, returns to her house and leads a "disconsolate life." Horatio, on the other hand, still unmarried, has applied himself strictly to his business and has, ironically, become rich and "sighs" when he hears Leonora's name but has made no charge against her ill conduct towards him.

In Chaucer's story, Troilus falls in love with Criseyde, tells Pandarus, who goes to Criseyde to convince her to fall in love with Troilus, which she is unable to do. In an unfortunate turn where she must go to Greece, she there sees and falls in love with Diomede and is charged with being unfaithful, "slyding in corage." Fielding's Horatio falls in love with Leonora, who, like Criseyde, falls in love with someone else. Unlike Criseyde, Leonora has made a promise to Horatio to marry him. Leonora's aunt, the parallel character to Pandarus, is unlike him in that she has no relation with Horatio, no conversation with him. She does, however, volunteer to tell him that Leonora has had her affections change. The aunt is like Pandarus to the extent that she influences the thinking of Leonora, but does so to change Leonora's affections. She sees that Leonora has fallen for Bellarmine, who is rich and cultured, and so she encourages these affections. Pandarus, on the other hand, tries to effect in Criseyde some affection for Troilus, an affection she does not really have. On the other hand, when she meets Diomede, she does indeed feel an attraction, an affection for him.

We are not sure of Leonora's affections for Horatio because it is he who makes such strong overtures to her and she is swept up by him and his overtures. But when she sees Bellarmine, she is very conscious and articulate about her feelings for him. Fielding gives the kind of detail, uses the kind of language, rhetoric, which explicates and elaborates in fine-grained detail the workings of Leonora's consciousness. Fielding uses the rhetoric of point of view to approach Leonora from a variety of ways.

He begins by saying that she is eighteen, tall, sprightly and well-shaped and asserts that this "beauty is less apt to deceive than allure; the good-humour which it indicates being often mistaken for good nature, and the vivacity for true understanding."

And so Horatio, at a dance one evening, whispers to Leonora that he "is desirous to take a turn or two with her in private . . . for he had something to communicate to her of great consequence . . . the whole future of his happiness depended on it."

Leonora agrees and "very much suspected what was coming" and wants to "defer it til another time." But she finally agrees to walk with him, during which time, he asks her to marry him; he asks her for her name. But again, it is the rhetoric Fielding uses to communicate the request that explicates intention and motivation formation and execution. Horatio is "trembling and pale," "sighing deeply" as he speaks, and "looking on her with a tenderness unimaginable and speaking with a "faltering accent." The suggestion then of the rhetoric is one of sincerity while the rhetoric for Leonora suggests falsity. She appears to give one impression but does not intend that impression. He asserts, as does Troilus of Criseyde, that his future happiness depends on her. She is surprised by this as is Criseyde, who, realises the power she has over Troilus. Leonora "blushes" and "with an angry look as she can possibly put on" suspected that this is what he was going to say and wanted to return immediately to the dance as she herself was now beginning to tremble. The reader is unsure of Leonora's feelings. Why is the "anger put on?" Does she really feel something for Horatio and is attempting to repress, suppress it?

Horatio, then, unsuccessful with the rhetoric of speech and personal contact, decides to write her a letter, using the rhetoric of the written word with which to express his affections, intentions and desires. In it, he mourns her absence since she is the object of his devotion. He writes about the dissatisfaction of the society to which he is accustomed—the society of learned men of wit. His sentiments for her, which he says are delicate and must be kept hidden because they may sound ridiculous to his scholarly friends, are actually what give him the utmost rapture and contentment. He concludes his letter to her by saying that he has put all his energies in "hope." He hopes that Leonora will respond to his love because he wishes that "every action of his life will have the glorious satisfaction of conducing to her happiness." The greatest happiness for him consists in being with her and making her happy.

Leonora, unlike Criseyde who did not want to "put anything in writing," also responds with a letter. She is impressed by the "refinement of his mind," and the "delicate sentiments expressed there." She is amazed that she is the object of such motivations—that Horatio is only interested in making her happy. She agrees that "domestick cares are sweetened by the pleasing consideration that the man on earth who best deserves, to reap profit and pleasure from all she does." She too is frustrated by conversation with women as he is by his men of wit and learning. She feels led by inclination to love him but her judgement forces her to condemn him because of his poverty.

The change occurs when she sees Bellarmine's coach pass by and falls in love with "that equipage." She is like Criseyde, who, when she saw Troilus pass by in all his military regalia, felt her heart flutter. The difference is that Criseyde already knew from Pandarus that Troilus loved her and so Criseyde realises that she has power over *this* particular powerful warrior and soldier. Her love, her infatuation, her palpitations of heart at the sight of him are mixed with this power motive. Part of the love is motivated by the fact that "he is wonderful to love; he is a wonderful object of love; he is an object to be conquered." Comparable to Troilus' military power is the power of Bellarmine's wealth.

At a dance, an "assembly," in the evening, Leonora had "intended to pay her dear Horatio the compliment of refusing to dance in his absence" but as the attractive Bellarmine arrived and everyone took note of him, so did Leonora. When Bellarmine saw Leonora, he stood "motionless and fixed like a statue" such that everyone in the room knew where his admiration rested. The Criseyde-like power struggle arises in Leonora when she realises that she is indeed admired by this attractive, rich man and is the envy of every woman present and it is at this that her heart flutters and her head agitates with convulsion. She had never tasted anything like this "happiness." She then proceeds to distort her person with a thousand childish tricks. Her word, her behaviours, her laughter, her carriage were as absurd as her desires which, at this point, were to "affect an insensibility of the stranger's admiration" and at the same time a triumph that she had achieved it. She then proceeded to dance with him all night and felt "perhaps the highest pleasures, which she was capable of feeling." Leonora did not sleep that night but dreamt of this fine man, his clothes and his "equipage."

What Horatio achieved with "sighs and tears, love and tenderness, so long in obtaining," Bellarmine achieved in an instant with "gallantry and gaiety." Bellarmine's impudence demolishes in a few hours Horatio's modesty during a full year of waiting.

Obviously, Leonora cannot avoid thinking about Horatio and her promises to him and she wishes that she had not seen the "charming Bellarmine" and his "charming equipage." Horatio is indeed to be her husband and lover but Bellarmine is also far "genteeler, handsomer and finer." Her dialogue with herself proceeds: "Why is it that yesterday, I loved only Horatio and today I don't?" She concludes that it is because she has now seen Bellarmine. She fears now that she is going to break Horatio's heart but she also sees that she can break Bellarmine's heart as well. But Horatio was promised first. But Bellarmine chose her of all the women in the assembly. Horatio had never shown her this kind of attention and affection. Horatio could never give her what (attention and equipage) Bellarmine could. In marrying Bellarmine, she will be the envy of all. She does not want to sacrifice herself to Horatio merely because she is afraid he will die without her.

The next morning at breakfast, Leonora's aunt, her own Pandarus, advises her to take Bellarmine while the taking is there and forget Horatio. The aunt advises that Leonora should take advantage of "what fortune has thrown her way." Leonora reminds her aunt of her engagement to Horatio and the aunt says that she should thank heaven that she still has power to break it. How could she possibly hesitate, insists the aunt, when Bellarmine's riches are compared with Horatio's poverty. Leonora will love in luxury and contentment the rest of her life. The choice, to the aunt, is obvious. Like Criseyde, Leonora is worried about what "the world" will say, but Leonora's aunt counters with the fact that the world will honor her for being so prudent and not entering into a binding contract too soon. The aunt's philosophy of life is based upon money, power and prestige. If someone wants to be successful, they must have money. And besides, Horatio is just a university fellow while Bellarmine is a fine gentleman just come from many travels.

The aunt then volunteers to "disengage" Leonora from Horatio so that Leonora won't have the unpleasant task of doing so herself, but Horatio comes in unexpectedly on Bellarmine and Leonora, who were engaged in a "polite discourse" about his possessions and "liveries." Horatio apologises for interrupting; Bellarmine traverses the room, humming. Horatio takes Leonora aside and asks her, not "out of jealousy," who this man was. She is taken aback by his raising the question of jealousy. She wonders why Horatio would even be concerned about who he was and why he would ever be jealous. She acts as if there is nothing between them, as if he were some stranger who just walked into the room. Bellarmine walks up to them and says that he feels that he might be intruding on some private conversation and is going to leave but Leonora insists there is nothing private occurring. Horatio wonders who this man is who Leonora so freely admits to the "secrecy" of their relationship. She insists that there are no secrets between them of any great consequence and she is quite "indifferent" to his visit and wonders why he is so ill-bred as to insist on remaining when he sees that she is otherwise engaged. To her, Horatio is a "common acquaintance who has laid aside the ceremonies of good breeding." Horatio feels as if he is in a dream; he wonders why Leonora does not recall what has passed between them, at which point Bellarmine comes to her defense.

The aunt fortuitously enters the room at this time and assures Horatio that he is not in a dream. Leonora has had an "alteration in her affections" at which point Leonora bursts into tears. Horatio challenges Bellarmine to a duel. The aunt tells Leonora not to worry about Horatio; he wouldn't do anything serious. But Leonora awakens the next morning to news that Horatio had "run him through." She "leapt out of bed, danced about the room in a frantic manner, tore her hair and beat her breast in the agonies of despair." The aunt tried to comfort her by telling her that as long as Bellarmine was still alive, there was hope that his wounds would heal and all her languishing and affliction would do him no good. And if Bellarmine succumbs, then she should endeavor to regain her affection for Horatio.

But she is too disgusted with her own duplicity and the pain she has caused all the way round. She then turns on the aunt and accuses the aunt of taking advantage of her "youth and simplicity" and forcing her to lose her dear Horatio. The aunt still is convinced that she did the best thing for Leonora by recommending that she forget Horatio and go with Bellarmine.

Bellarmine, more devoted than ever, writes to her from his hospital bed. The duel has actually fuelled his devotion. He is now in a contest to "win" her.

And with this news, Leonora is restored to contentment, reconciled with her aunt and forgotten Horatio. Leonora's passion for Bellarmine returned with a greater force and she resolved, against the advice of her aunt, to go visit him and minister to him, giving "unbridled indulgence to her passion." It should be noted that the word "passion" is used with regard to her feelings for Bellarmine while the word "affection" is used in reference to Horatio suggesting a significant difference in each relationship. "Passion" suggests something uncontrolled, irrational while the word "affection" is often used to suggest something more intimate, real and sincere.

Everyone began to talk about Leonora's conduct, her constant ministrations to the wounded Bellarmine, and she was very severely censured in these sessions. Leonora's father now becomes involved in her personal affairs. He receives an anonymous letter, in an unknown woman's hand, saying how basely Leonora has been acting, how cruelly she treated Horatio. The character sketch of the father is also interesting. He is a man who looks upon Leonora as an "unhappy consequence of youthful pleasures." In the world's language, he passed as a good father because he worked very hard to provide for his children's material needs. But he also heaped up money for its own sake and looked on his children as rivals. The father felt that Bellarmine would be a good match for Leonora, as did the aunt, because of Bellarmine's person, equipage, family and estate, but when Bellarmine wanted the father to give him Leonora's share of the estate after they married and the father said that she would not get her share until after he died, Bellarmine decided not to match with Leonora and to tell her that her father was unwilling to give him her hand in marriage which he writes to her in a letter from France saying that she might "well guess his manner of refusing me." An interesting rhetorical turn of phrase suggesting "like father, like daughter," to the extent that all the way round each of these people is more concerned about money first than anything else. Even though he loved her with all his heart, he could not marry her without any fortune. The father merely said that he had a lot of expenses on projects at this time and had great expectations for them. They had not yet produced anything.

Leonora received this news poorly and continued to be the subject of conversation generally and ridicule in particular. She returns to a rather disconsolate life, having neither Horatio nor Bellarmine and deserves more pity than condemnation or ridicule that she had lost the good Horatio. The story ends with the ironic twist that, in his dejection, the poor Horatio devoted himself singlemindedly to his business and thus amassed a considerable fortune and so became rich, never hearing Leonora's name, except to sigh nor has he uttered one syllable to charge her with ill conduct towards him.

Sarah and Maurice

In Graham Greene's novel *The End of the Affair*, the lover, Maurice Bendrix is motivated to have his partner in the affair, Sarah Miles, followed by a private investigator because he does not trust her. He himself is aware of the irony here since their very affair began in dishonesty with Sarah's act of mistrust towards her husband.

Bendrix philosophises that such jealousy and mistrust that he is experiencing, a jealousy and mistrust that would hire a private investigator to follow the beloved, is motivated not only by an apparent love but also by something deeper, some desire, yearning. Bendrix wonders about the fury of his love, his desire, his jealousy, and when he thinks of himself as having been a "lover" of Sarah, who is married to Henry, his "will travels irresistibly back to the point where pain began,"[9] where intention and act were formed and executed. Unlike Troilus and Criseyde or Leonora, Horatio, and Bellarmine, the relationship between Sarah and Maurice arises *after* they both formed intentions to commit themselves to others.

There was one week between their "first fumbling kiss" and a real date where they went out together to dinner and a movie. The movie was a film version of one of Bendrix' books. Bendrix "told himself" that he was making this date partly to show off, partly as a courtesy after the kiss, and partly out of interest in the married life of the civil servant Henry Miles, Sarah's husband. He realises later in the novel the fragility of these excuses, especially the pretense of "interviewing" Sarah with a view to the writing of his next novel. Suggesting

---

[9] Graham Greene, *The End of the Affair*. (New York; Penguin Books, 1962), p. 42.

that Henry, the husband, accompany them was also one of those "politenesses" which would help him avoid the fact that there is an interest in an affair here.

The movie itself is an interesting synecdoche. As the film version of his book rolls past, Bendrix continually asserts to Sarah throughout the viewing that "that's not what I wrote," until which time he is "suddenly and unexpectedly" removed from the stock cliches of the film which had twisted his true intent in the novel into a dialogue in a small scene in a cheap restaurant which he says is actually what genuinely moved him. Book, film and reality blend in a novel.

In the scene in the movie, the lover orders steak and onions but the girl hesitates because her husband does not like the smell of onions. Whereupon, the lover is hurt and angry, realising that the girl is going to return to the inevitable embrace of her husband at home.

Bendrix watches this film version of his own writing, admires the success of the scene to the extent that it moved him so unexpectedly, and wants to return home and re-read it. It seemed to convey that sense of passion in a single episode to him (hence synecdochic) without any rhetoric and it worked. He was very happy and proud of his own writing.

The dinner scene between the two lovers in Greene's novel parallels the dinner scene between the two lovers in Bendrix' novel and then the film. The scene itself, and the onions in particular, become synecdochic, singularly representative.

Bendrix and Sarah have the same conversation as the lovers in the movie. Sarah's husband also cannot tolerate the smell of onions. Bendrix says that it was at this moment that he "fell in love." He says that he's not exactly sure if it's the onions or the woman or her frankness but they proceeded to hold hands under the table, enjoy the food and leave for Maiden Lane where they reprised the kiss and declared their love:

> I said, "I'm in love."
> "Me, too."
> "We can't go home."
> "No."
>   (p. 44)

So they went to a hotel. Again, Bendrix remembers those isolated, trivial details, some of which become synecdochic. He recalls the manager and the cost of the room but not how Sarah looked or what they did, except that they were both very nervous and made love badly. He concludes: "It doesn't really matter. We had started—that was the point." And so his jealousy started as well.

At Sarah's home (p. 45), they have a drink together with her husband Henry, who admires Bendrix' ability to write—his power at putting things down in words. For some reason, Bendrix here likes, admires Henry. The convolution, the confusing admixture of love and hate, jealousy and desire begin here and as he kisses Sarah again at the door, she senses a "meaning behind the kiss, the whisper in the brain" (45) and asks what the matter is, to which he responds "nothing" and assures her that he will call her in the morning. She says it would be better if she called him. The jealousy then begins when he realises "how well she knew how to conduct an affair like this;" how cautious she was; how she knew the exact stair that squeaked when Henry walked down them.

Because Sarah had broken trust and love with her husband, Bendrix wonders how she could love him and how she can be trusted. They thus begin and consent to their "affair" knowing that it will have an ending because the love vowed in the marriage is the love that is intended to be for the lifetime and is less likely to end. The affair, like the story of the affair, or any story or activity, begins *in medias res*, and the key point that I am trying to make in this book by using these examples from literature is that care needs to be taken in examining the motivations, desires, attitudes, feelings, intentions that bring one to a particular decision and literature, language, assists this process.

The lives of Sarah and Henry Miles, Maurice Bendrix, Troilus and Criseyde, Leonora, Horatio, and Bellarmine are indeed irrevocably changed by their decisions. What may appear to be a seemingly inconsequential action or decision like Sarah and Maurice having an affair or Troilus and Criseyde getting married are in effect actions and decisions that depend heavily on adequate examination of and formation of intention and motivation. In using these pieces of literature, I have attempted to illustrate how language facility, literacy, is a key element in this process. The devices of vocabulary, rhetoric, linguistics, sentence structure, grammar, any and all the tools of language, are effective in the discovery of, the formation of and the communication of intentions, desires, motivations, attitudes, beliefs. Conclusive sentences like "I want to marry" or "I want to leave this city" or "I want to have an affair," need to be the result of or dictate the rigorous examination of the forces, motivations, intentions and attitudes on which they are based.

Maurice and Sarah and Henry certainly parallel Leonora, Bellarmine, and Horatio, or Troilus, Criseyde, and Diomede in any discussion of the formation of love relationships and intentions to marry. However, the Maurice sequence in Greene's novel has the additional aspect of the writer seeing himself in his work, his novel made into a movie and the scene in the movie paralleling his actual dinner with Sarah. There are a number of different intersections here that allow Maurice to see his affair with Sarah differently. Thomas DeQuincey has similar intersections in his re-consideration and re-membering why he left Manchester, with which story I shall conclude this chapter.

But before proceeding to the DeQuincey section, I would like to conclude this section with a quotation from George Eliot's novel *Adam Bede*, which also has a "triangle" relationship. Hetty Sorrel is pregnant by Arthur Donnithorne. Adam is infatuated with Hetty but doesn't know about the pregnancy or Arthur. Hence, the following:

> Not a word was spoken as they [Hetty and Adam] gathered currants. Adam's heart was too full to speak, and he thought Hetty knew all that was in it. She was not indifferent to his presence after all; she blushed when she saw him, and then there was that touch of sadness about her which must surely mean love, since it was the opposite of her usual manner, which had often impressed him as indifference. And he could glance at her continually as she bent over the fruit, while the level evening sunbeams stole through the thick apple-tree boughs and rested on her round cheek and neck as if they too were in love with her. It was to Adam...the time when he believes that the first woman he has ever loved betrays by slight something, a word, a tone, a glance, the quivering of a lip or an eyelid, that she is at least beginning to love him in return. The sign is so slight, it is scarcely perceptible to the ear or eye—he could describe it to no one—it is a mere feather-touch, yet is seems to have changed his whole being, to have merged an uneasy yearn-

ing into a delicious unconsciousness of everything but the present moment...But the first glad moment in our first love is a vision which returns to us to the last, and brings with it a thrill of feeling intense and special . . . his own emotion as he looked at her and believed that she was thinking of him, and that there was no need for them to talk . . . . And Hetty? You know quite well that Adam was mistaken about her. Like many other men, he thought the signs of love for another were signs of love toward himself . . . . she was absorbed as usual in thinking and wondering about Arthur's possible return . . . the anxieties and fears of a first passion, with which she was trembling, had become stronger with vanity, had given her for the first time that sense of helpless dependence on another's feeling . . . For the first time Hetty felt that there was something soothing to her in Adam's timid yet manly tenderness: she wanted to be treated lovingly—O, it was very hard to bear this blank of absence, silence, apparent indifference, after those moments of flowing love! . . . Hetty, we know, was not the first woman that had behaved more gently to the man who loved her in vain, because she had herself begun to love another. It was a very old story; but Adam knew nothing about it, so he drank in the sweet delusion.[10]

Thomas DeQuincey

He left Manchester in 1802 at 17 years of age, wrote the first narrative of the leaving in 1821 at 36 years of age, and then revised it and expanded it in 1856 at 71 years of age. These re-readings and re-visions of the narrative indicate my earlier point that individuals' words and behaviours return to them and become new "inputs." They read, as if for the first time, their intentional/behavioural structures and interpret or re-interpret themselves differently at different points and places in time. It is also important to note that DeQuincey "creates himself," much like Chaucer and Greene do with their characters. As

---

[10] George Eliot, *Adam Bede*, (London: Penguin Books, 1985), 265–267.

DeQuincey observes his own behaviour and re-reads his own writings, these return to him as new inputs by which he can re-structure, re-organise, re-conceptualise himself and his intentional states.

In the first narration, he says that this act of leaving "colored his entire life"[11] and that is why he remembers the morning so clearly. He awoke at 3:30 A.M. and gazed out at the collegiate church. He knew that this was the right decision for him because he said that he was "firm and immovable in his purpose" but at the same time "agitated [quite naturally] by anticipation of uncertain dangers and troubles." The "deep peace" of the morning contrasted with his agitation and was medicinal for him, he writes. The silence quieted his spirit. He dressed and lingered in the room for a moment because this room was his "pensive citadel" for nearly a year and half which time he remembers as "happy hours" in the midst of a "general dejection" and sadness in his relations with his guardian. He writes that he wept as he looked about for the last time on this room. He remembers and sees this morning "distinctly as if it were yesterday," especially the picture of the lovely lady whose "radiant, tranquil and divine countenance," hung over the mantelpiece and gave him many hours of consolation, as if she were his "patron saint." He concludes the narration by writing that as the clock struck four he kissed the portrait and left the room "forever." The verbal structure mediates the behavioural simply when it indicates that he awoke early, lingered and finally left. But the verbal structure also mediates an intentional-motivational state which was apprehensive, fearful and sad.

Thirty five years later, in 1856, he re-wrote the episode and expanded it. At the point in the first narration where he remembered that he had spent many "happy hours" in this room, he was prompted to write, 35 years later, that it was "certain that [he] ever again . . . should enjoy hours *as* happy?"[12] He realises in retrospect that he might have "receded from his plan" but in terms of how he felt then, no alternatives were available except to leave.

---

[11] Thomas DeQuincey, *The Confessions of an English Opium-Eater and Other Writings*, edited with an introduction by Grevel Lindop, (Oxford University Press, 1985), 9.

[12] Thomas DeQuincey, *Selected Writings of Thomas DeQuincey* selected and edited with an introduction by Philip Van Doren Stern, (New York: The Modern Library, 1937), 687.

He adds a major section to the narrative due to the fact that he remembers that he was dejected about leaving (a new neurochemical transmission which causes a past event to change), and he tells a story within the original story when he adds that he was apparently thrown into a trancelike state, a dream-like reverie of what I have been calling these illocutionary forces or neurochemical transmissions, during which he had a "hateful remembrance" of something that happened two years earlier. The illocutionary forces constitute a performative, a wholly internal activity later written out as another performative, this narrative. The written words of the published narrative become the "constative" in the sense that they establish as an external, objective fact (as a phenomenological object, Husserl's "bracket") an internal, subjective reality, an activity, a performative.

My point in using these dual narrations, written 35 years apart, is to illustrate the overlap and intersection of experiences and perceptions in the mind, which I have attempted to elaborate theoretically and philosophically, in earlier chapters. At the time that he left in 1802, he was seventeen years old and probably somewhat confused and anxious about getting out on his own. But as the writer of the narrative, nineteen years later, at 36 years of age, he is more keenly aware of the actual sadness that he felt at having to leave; and as the reviser and editor of the narration, 35 years later at over 70 years of age, he remembers another connection, this "hateful experience" of two years earlier, when he was 15, which he joins with the leaving at seventeen and uses to explain the dejection. These intersecting transitions and references in the intentional structure of DeQuincey's consciousness are mediated to others by the verbal structure of the narrative.

The hateful experience that he remembers is a visit to the Whispering Gallery at Saint Paul's Cathedral in London. At Saint Paul's, he remembers first standing "on the very spot" where Lord Nelson is buried and where the "many flags captured from France, Spain, and Holland" are "pompously floating." Lord Nelson's tomb and the flags of the conquered countries make him think that in the "chance and change amongst mighty nations, . . . fatality [might] often attend an evil choice." That is, when a nation elects to make war upon another nation and if the challenge is accepted, each is confronted with the possibility of defeat.

These flags and the reflections then make DeQuincey think of the "Roman warning, *Nescit vox missa reverti*, (that a word once uttered is irrevocable)," which passage I locate as the key moment of insight into intentional-motivational structure and intention formation evidenced in the narrative, and a primary force in DeQuincey's intentional structure. The 70 year old DeQuincey connects these words of the Roman warning with his leaving Manchester such that they cause him to realise that both his intention to leave and the act of leaving Manchester are irrevocable. They are equal actions and if the interior/intentional is not in harmony with the behavioural, there could be problems later because both are "irrevocable." In other words, if he did not really want to leave, intend to leave, then that sentiment, that force, will remain with him throughout his life. At the time, he *had* to leave, but in retrospect, at 70 years of age, he is aware of the future fatalities that attended his decision. At 70 years of age, he reads what he wrote at 35 about an experience he had when he was seventeen and this act of reading returns to him as a new trace, becomes a new input, a new perception, which causes him to remember a visit to Saint Paul's Cathedral when he was fifteen and he reinterprets that visit in the light of leaving Manchester and his narrative account of leaving. Past, present and future intersect in his consciousness in this narrative in such a way that there is no past, present or future. An event at 15 becomes lost, forgotten, relegated to the "unconscious" until which time it is re-touched, made conscious, when DeQuincey re-reads his narrative. At 70 years of age, he is also 15 years old visiting the Gallery, 17 years old leaving Manchester, and 35 years old writing the narrative of the leaving and feeling inexplicably dejected. And he is making a significant point about a person's interior, intentional life: it is that there are forces there that often echo irrevocably, coincidentally; external activities and behaviours are events which have been frozen irrevocably in time and if the intentional, interior forces were not in harmony, that disharmony is frozen and echoes in the mind, plagues the conscience.

The act of re-reading at 70 the narrative that he wrote at 35 of his leaving Manchester causes him to re-interpret the leaving in terms of the earlier visit to Saint Paul's Cathedral when he was 15 years old. The verbal structure returns to him as a prompt to his Dretskean "internal indicator" and triggers a new response, a new interpretation and some new thoughts about intention formation.

Recall also Eckartsburg's mapping of consciousness diagram to which I referred in Chapter Two, pp 51–52.

The visit to Saint Paul's and the Whispering Gallery was not a once for all, irrevocable, event. The fullness of the experience of visiting the Cathedral is completed in this act of re-writing the Manchester narrative. The behaviour of visiting Saint Paul's and the behaviour of leaving Manchester are not complete acts until he re-interprets, re-edits, and re-writes them 35 years later. These behaviours also juxtapose in a nexus of exemplification, a gestalt of interrelations of interior forces (performatives) and exterior events (constatives) expressed in words (a performative-constative). DeQuincey communicates in this narrative part of the nexus of intentional forces which represent the innate language and discourse in the intentional structure in his consciousness.

His central, albeit absolute, realisation with regard to his having left Manchester (when he sees the flags of the conquered countries) that "once a word is uttered it is irrevocable" is re-inforced when he goes to the Whispering Gallery in the Cathedral itself. There he remembers experiencing the full impact of the Roman proverb, although at the time he was not aware of this fullness. His friend breathed a "solemn but unacceptable truth" in the "softest whispers" at one end of the Gallery and it "reached [DeQuincey] as a deafening menace in tempestuous uproars." As a 15 year old, this was an interesting, new experience during a day-long excursion of the sights of London. But as a 70 year old writer, editing the narrative of the day he left Manchester, the experience of visiting the Cathedral rings with a resonance and clairvoyance that connects in a shocking kind of way to DeQuincey's leaving and explains his dejection.

His decision to leave and his act of leaving Manchester were a decision and an act that he now perceives in retrospect as "echoing back" with a "tempestuous uproar" because it was, apparently, to a certain extent, an "unacceptable decision" which influenced the entire course of his life, and as it echoes back unacceptably, it is irrevocable, it can't be changed. At 70, he remembers and knows that even at 15, he had made wrong decisions and was ashamed of some of his judgments; idle hopes, false admirations or contempts with which he had sympathised and which he had "pronounced" but at 15 had subsequently ignored and forgot about; but at 70 they run down the corridors of his mind with a deafening menace and a tempestuous uproar—unchangeable, irrevocable. His leaving that house placed a Rubicon between himself and a possible return, he says, and this decision may not be one that is altogether approved in his secret heart and the lingering in the room is not only a mourning of the passing of happy hours but an attempt by the "sullen whispers" of his conscience" to speak in "volleying thunders" 50 years later.

In the expanded version of the narrative, he says that a "sudden step upon the stair broke up [his] dream," as opposed to the clock striking four in the earlier narrative. And since he re-writes the narrative with this extended interior monologue as a meditative addition, he changed (fictionalised) the clock to strike six instead of four in the later edition. In the first narrative he was in the room a half-hour and in the second narrative he was in the room two hours and a half, after which he bids a hasty farewell because he might change his mind and stay, something he could not do at the time but in retrospect might have been the better decision.

DeQuincey's behavioural act of leaving Manchester becomes a language act when he writes the narrative of it 19 years later at 35 years of age and then an intentional act when he examines the motivations behind the act in greater detail. There are three distinct activities or structures here: the behavioural, the mediatory or verbal, and the intentional: each becomes primary at different times.

The behaviours of visiting the Cathedral and Gallery and leaving Manchester are performatives, *de re* occurrences, observable, provable. He did leave Manchester on a particular day. The event is recorded in the verbal structure of the narrative but sprinkled with the reporting of the behaviour is also a report of intentions and motivations. The intentions and motivations are performatives. They are an accumulation of forces which find expression in language but, unlike the behaviour of leaving itself, the performance of the intentions and motivations can only be observed in the speaking or writing (as constative) of the person; thus, performatives. The behavioural act itself of re-reading, revising and re-editing the narrative is an activity which makes the verbal structure central, a phenomenological object whereby DeQuincey observes his own intentional, interior life as a constative, in language, and the behavioural structure of leaving is, to a certain extent, fictionalised in order to communicate the more important, significant truth of the intentional structure. He constitutes this internal activity in language. The language is a constative in the sense that it confirms and makes visible a hitherto invisible performance.

The final edition becomes what Brentano calls a "nexus of exemplification" of the interior, mental, causal relations and inferences in communion with the behavioural and verbal structures. The behaviours of visiting, leaving, reading and the intentions to visit, leave, write, re-read, and re-write are separate but related and can be considered causes of each other at various times. One structure becomes more central than others at a particular time. At 70, DeQuincey reads the narrative he wrote and *it* becomes the real world, the primary focus, whereas when he actually left Manchester, on the morning of his departure, the behavioural act itself, specifically the room itself, was the primary, real world, the central focus. It was only after the fact, many years later, that the intentional structure, the reasons for leaving, become the primary world. In terms of the rhetoric of the formation of intention, DeQuincey's narrative illustrates the centrality of the verbal structure, the language and rhetoric, in communication of intention and behaviour, and in so doing it accents the crucial need for individuals to be literate if they are to harmonise interior, intentional life with exterior, behavioural life. It also gives literacy a renewed significance as a rhetorical tool.

Chaucer and Fielding both describe love triangles with a third party intercessor; both attempt to deconstruct the formation of intention in their characters, but Fielding focuses more on the influences of class structure and money in the formation of the construct. Greene's triangle includes the fact that Maurice is a writer whose intention to have an affair with Sarah intersects with a book he has written—one made into the movie they see on their first date together. Thomas DeQuincey is also a writer who reviews a decision he made in his life by writing it out in his autobiography and then re–reading, re–considering in retrospect how the intention was formed. Reading and writing, then, are key influences in Maurice's and DeQuincey's formation of intention.

> . . . *we do not, normally, at least, find ourselves*
> *with intention; we form intentions.*
>
> H.P. Grice
> "Intention and Uncertainty," 1971

CHAPTER FIVE

From Theology: Religious Pluralism

"More tortuous than all else is the human heart,
beyond remedy; who can understand it?
I, the Lord, alone probe the Mind
and test the heart,
To reward everyone according to his ways,
according to the merit of his deeds."

Jeremiah 17, 10

To leap, at this point, to theology and religious pluralism in a book about formation of intentions may appear a glaring incoherence and certainly a serious error in structure and organisation. However, a key point in my discussion of formation of intentions is the multiplicity of forces that come into play. I have illustrated this multiplicity through examples from philosophy, biology, linguistics and literature and the rhetorics of these disciplines, and I now turn to the rhetoric of religion and theology as another way to illustrate that concepts are created, attitudes are assumed, and intentions are formed in a variety of ways and from a multiplicity of intersecting forces. Religion and theology are particularly interesting because they assume a unity, a singularity, and bury or deny any effects of multiplicity or plurality.

The first and more significant of the two biblical passages which I choose to begin my discussion of religious pluralism and theological multiplicity is the story of Pentecost, Acts 2: 1ff.

When the day of Pentecost came round, they had all met together when suddenly there came from heaven a sound as of a violent wind which filled the entire house in which they were sitting; and there appeared to them tongues as of fire; these separated and came to rest on the head of each of them; they were all filled with the Holy Spirit and began to speak in different languages as the Spirit gave them power to express themselves. Now there were devout men living in Jerusalem from every nation under heaven and at the sound they all assembled and each one was bewildered to hear these men speaking in his own language. They were amazed and astonished. Surely, they said, all these men speaking are Galilean? How does it happen that each of us hears them in his own native langauge? Parthians, Medes, Elamites; people from Mesopotamia, Judaea and Cappadocia, Pontus, and Asia, Phrygia, Pamphylia, Egypt and parts of Libya round Cyrene; residents of Rome—Jews and proselytes alike—Cretans and Arabs: we hear them preaching in our own language about the marvels of God. Everyone was amazed and perplexed; they asked one another what it all meant; Some, however, laughed it off "They have been drinking too much new wine," they said.

This passage, of course, has a forerunner, an analogue, in the Tower of Babel story in Genesis 11, but with a shift in focus. In Genesis, everyone speaks the same language and they take pride in this unity and they make sure that nothing will disturb their secure language system; no other languages and no other points of view. God says (I interpret) "I'd better straighten them out; the nature of their unity is in their variety, their multiplicity," so God creates a confusion of languages, ideas and points of view. The people then had to proceed with the difficult task of translation, of communication. There is no more the comfort of everybody understanding everyone else. They, and we by extension, need to do this work of translating ourselves, our ideas, our points of view, our experiences, our intentions and motives for others to understand and this goes beyond the mere problem of language, beyond mere French and English; it's cultural and ultimately deeply personal.

There are three principle literary images (fire, wind, language) used by the biblical writer of the *Acts of the Apostles* in the Pentecost story to figure forth unity in multiplicity. The principle of unity subsists in the movement of the Holy Spirit figured by the fire and wind, reminiscent of God breathing forth the word of life into Adam and later the word made flesh in the Son. The multiplicity is figured forth in the image of many languages.

The listeners were "amazed, perplexed, bewildered, astonished" at the apostles' ability to understand the foreign languages. This emotional reaction, it seems to me, is a consequence, a fact of life, about plurality and multiplicity in that they bewilder and confuse us and so we don't like them. We like everything neat, ordered, tidy and unified—the blessed rage for order. One way people try to bestow order and unity is by attaching a meaning or explanation to a series of otherwise chaotic events. They're just drunk, they're babbling, or less obvious, perhaps: there seems to be a unity here among these diverse, opposing elements. The comprehensive list of peoples, cultures, nations and races really reinforces the notion of plurality, and we of course could re-write the passage today and say "How does it happen that each of us hears them in his own native language—Sikhs, Quebeckers, aboriginals, Kuwaitis, Khurds, Italians, Muslims, Jews, Christians, abortionists, homosexuals, prostitutes."

The second biblical passage that I would like to use is from Chapter 12 of Paul's first letter to the Corinthians where he has what has become the classic image of plurality—his analogy with the body.

> Just as the human body, though it is made up of many parts, is a single unity because all these parts, though many, make one body, . . . nor is the body to be identified with any one of its many parts. If the foot were to say "I am not a hand so I do not belong" or if the ear were to say . . . or the eye . . . If the whole body were just one eye, how would you hear anything.

> Instead, God put all the separate parts into the body on purpose. If all the parts were the same, how could it be a body. As it is, the parts are many but the body is one. The eye cannot say to the hand "I do not need you" nor the head to the feet.

What is more, it is precisely the parts of the body that are weakest which are the indispensable ones; and the least honourable parts of the body that we clothe with the greatest care. So our improper parts get decorated in a way that our more proper parts do not need. God has arranged the body so that more dignity is given to the parts which are without it and so there may not be disagreements inside the body but that each part may be equally concerned for all the others. If one part is hurt, all parts are hurt with it. If one part is given special honor, all parts enjoy it.

Now you are together Christ's body; but each of you is a different part of it. In the church, God has given the first place to apostles, the second to prophets, the third to teachers; after them miracles, and after them the gift of healing, helpers, good leaders, those with many languages. Are all of them apostles, or all of them prophets or all of them teachers? Do they all have the gift of healing? Do all speak strange languages and all interpret them?

Paul then goes into his panegyric on love but I would like to double back to the verses that just precede, rather introduce, the analogy of the body section; verses that have become a hymn or an anthem and may have indeed served as a liturgical anthem for the Corinthian community. But whether or not they did, the verses stand apart as exceptionally beautiful and poetic; one of those times when the richness of Paul's langauge, with the assistance of translators, rises to new heights:

There is a variety of gifts but always the same Spirit; there are all sorts of service to be done but always the same Lord; working in all sorts of different ways in different people, it is the same God who is working in all of them. The particular way in which the Spirit is given to each person is for a good purpose. One may have the gift of preaching with wisdom given him by the Spirit; another may have the gift of preaching instruction given him by the Spirit; and another the gift of faith given him by the same Spirit; another again the gift of healing, through the one Spirit; one, the power of miracles, another prophecy; another the gift of recognising spirits; another the gift of tongues and another the ability to interpret them. All these are the work of the same Spirit, who distributes gifts to different people . . . .

And as the gospel of John says, "the wind blows where it will and we do not know where it comes from nor where it is going" (John 3:8). If Paul says that faith is a gift of the Spirit which some people have and others do not, then he assumes that some members of the church do not have faith; they may have another gift. We are encouraged not only to welcome people who have different ways of expressing, practising and experiencing their faith but we welcome people who do not even have faith and not with a view to giving them faith *vis-a-vis* hard-sell evangelism, but allowing the gift or gifts that they do have to emerge in the community.

Paul attributes plurality and unity to God's will, just as in the Tower of Babel story, there are separate, diverse parts of one thing because God made the thing that way. Paul's elaboration of the weakest part of the body, the one in pain, the one which is hurt, or even the one receiving special honor is of course the high point of the extended metaphor simply because it connects so strongly with the essential paradox of the Christian life—where there is weakness then *that* is the strength. In death is resurrection; in suffering is salvation. He who saves his life, loses it. If you would save your life, give it away. T.S. Eliot's Becket says "I am not in danger, only near to death."

But of course the analogy with the body limps because if we start to think in terms of improper and proper parts that need to be clothed because of their greater and lesser dignity, we run into problems. We need to keep Paul's point clearly in focus that as we look around our churches, our various communities and institutions of which we are a part, we see their multiple members as parts of those bodies, those communities. Some are honourable, some are improper, some are in disagreement, some are hurt, weak, not just physically weak, in need of hospitalization, crippled, aged, infirm, but emotionally, psychologically weak. And here is where I would like to extend Paul's analogy of the body to the mind, the psyche, in a Jungian sense. In our minds, in each of our individual psyches, there is an infinite multiplicity of desire, feeling, thought, attitude, motivation, intention—the biochemistry itself is multiple, constantly interacting, neurochemically energised, in one brain encased in one skull. Some parts may die in stroke. Some people are more rational, reasoned, scientific while others are more emotional, psychic, intuitive; some parts of the brain are stronger, weaker, dispensable, honourable, improper. Thomas DeQuincey's palimpsest image mirrors the brain function.

Paul ends his analogy by returning to the multiplicity of gifts in the body of Christ, the church, and lists them in a hierarchical order, bestowing on the multiplicity Paul's idea of unity—apostles first, prophets, second, then teachers, then miracle workers, helpers, linguists, translators, interpreters in an apparent descending order. I would guess that this is part of the biblical foundation for the present Roman Catholic hierarchical ordering from pope to Curia to cardinal to archbishop to bishop, priest, deacon etc. but this hierarchical, descending order was changed at Vatican II from the pyramid structure of descending order to the circular structure of collegial communion of groups in conversation around and with the pope. I extend the circular, collegial image from the image of a series of circles around the pope to a sociological matrix of overlapping, dissecting, interacting circles with different centres, and I extend this collegial image to that of a person attempting to form an intention.

And I think Paul's elaboration of gifts needs to be adapted simply in the naming: the apostles are bishops and priests and the prophets, healers and teachers could certainly be groups of lay persons. My personal perception of a major change which might come sooner than women priests or married priests is in the area of preaching ministry, homiletics and instruction. I think that this ministry needs to be extended beyond the ordained hierarchy. The charism, the gift, of preaching can be given to anyone, notably deacons who have been set aside, ordained to care for the Word while the priest is set aside, ordained, to be the minister of the Eucharist. The bishop is primary pastor and overseer of the gifts and their use in the community.

Pre-Vatican II is a hierarchical-descending order; the catholicity, the unity, is in the hierarchical ordering of the pluralities by power. Post-Vatican II is a collegial-circular ordering: the Catholicity, the unity, is in the circular ordering of the pluralities by priests re-distributing the power more democratically. The post-modern, the 21st century, holds forth a unity *in* plurality; a plurality of collegial-circular formations with indeterminate, varied centres. The catholicity, the unity, is in the multiple ordering of the pluralities in an ever-changing matrix as the centres of authority change. And so it is with formation of intention. Depending upon the circumstances, the collegial arrangement of desires, motives, attitudes and beliefs, a centre of authority for intention will change and vary. I do not mean this to be interpreted as an "anything goes" morality, a situation ethics. I mean that within a particular centre of commitment like marriage, other centres of intentional authority can emerge but not destroy the marriage commitment. The marriage commitment may be deconstructed and reconstructed in new ways.

I would like to discuss Bernard Lonergan's 1971 volume entitled *Doctrinal Pluralism* in which he considers the problem of the one and the many in terms of doctrine, like others have done in terms of morality. He argues that there may indeed be one, true, absolute doctrine but there are multiple ways of presenting it which depend on cultural, social, and political history. Lonergan writes that the multiplicity, plurality, is a concept rooted in history while unity, oneness is a concept rooted in philosophy, metaphysics.[1] Permanence or oneness are mysteries which transcend time and space, human investigation, intelligence and history. By its very nature, the concept of permanence stands above and beyond the created intellect and history.

But pluralism, multiplicity of interpretation and perspective are indeed rooted in time, space, creation, cultural-historical development and the key way that the created intellect grasps pluralism or multiplicity is through recognition of difference. Moral, religious, dogmatic, social-political, even philosophical difference takes place as a differentiating, a differentiation in consciousness, in the mind. Lonergan lists common sense, science, scholarship, intentionality analysis and faith with prayer as his principle components in a process of differentiating in consciousness.[2]

And, as I have written in previous chapters, Jacques Derrida really captures this idea of a differentiating consciousness. My reading of Derrida has significantly influenced my thinking about plurality and oneness, unity in diversity,

---

[1] Bernard Lonergan, *Doctrinal Pluralism*, The 1971 Pere Marquette Theology Lecture, (Milwaukee: Marquette University Press, 1971), 30.

[2] Lonergan, 56.

theological and moral relativism. Although Derrida is not explicitly religious in his writing; that is, his work does not concern theological-religious themes, scholars like Rudolf Bultmann and Lonergan have connected the idea of *differance*[3] to biblical-religious studies. Derrida has had more influence in the world of literature, but his ideas can also be applied to a discussion of church. There is a plurality, a diversity, a multiplicity of *difference* within the one church.

Basically, quite simply, Derrida's *differance* can be reduced to a consideration of the letters of the alphabet; they each mean something only to the extent that they stand as different from, but connected to other letters. This conceptualisation is then expanded to sentences, paragraphs, essays, books, ideas, doctrines, dogmas, laws and intention formation. An object stands as meaningful when in relation to something else and different from it.

If everything means something only to the extent that it is different from something else, these multiple things can be deconstructed, re-arranged, and reconstructed in a new way with new sets of differences. Jesuit Father Walter Ong says that this re-interpretation, or reconstructing, is not a mere relativism and most of us do fear the moral relativism of situation ethics but he says it is a "constructive relationality"[4]: a re-construction of differences in a new relation. Derrida implies for me that these deconstructions and reconstructions are part of the natural life processes.

In his article "In Praise of Pluralism," Ronald Thiemann addresses just this problem of moral relativity. He makes the interesting distinction between absolute truth and good and relativity of justification.[5] In other words, it is true that any action can be justified—moral relativism and situation ethics do indeed exist—but the justification systems are centred around an absolute truth or good. I am not a moralist and I don't want to discuss cases here, but there could be a minimum of two levels of multiple conversation: one about the morality of a particular case—an act by a particular person—and another about moral prin-

---

[3] Jacques Derrida, *Margins of Philosophy*, (The University of Chicago Press, 1972), 17.

[4] Walter Ong, "Realizing Catholicism: Faith, Learning and the Future," (*Theology Digest* 37: 4, Winter, 1990), 337.

[5] Ronald F. Thiemann, "In Praise of Pluralism," (*The Thomist*, Volume 53, 1989), 494.

ciples generally and questions about good and evil and truth quite apart from particular concrete situations even to the creation of specific, fictional examples simply to provoke the mind to play with the idea. On the level of dogma, conversations are carried on about the principle or idea of infallibility and another conversation about particular infallible statements or possible statements.

Thiemann goes on to consider moral conversations in our time as part of a *bricolage*,[6] a larger conversation in the social, political, cultural arenas. He argues that theologians have effectively marginalised themselves out of the conversation because their language, the terms they use, are inaccessible to people in other disciplines. And of course this argument could be transferred across the board of academic disciplines—disciplines need to make their language, their glossaries, accessible to other disciplines for any conversation to occur— reminiscent of the Tower of Babel—the disciplines need to retain and nourish their own language but need to continue to work at communicating with other disciplines so that each does not become myopically encased in its own system. *Bricolage* is a wonderful word which captures this idea of interdiscipline. Jack Goody in his anthropological treatise *The Domestication of the Savage Mind* develops this idea of the *bricoleur*,[7] which he got from anthropologist Claude Levi-Strauss, as one who is fluent and conversant in a variety of cultures and languages, one who disciplines his talent for cross-conversing as he accumulates a morality—a moral *bricoleur* is one whose moral expertise consists of his ability to discuss morality at different social-political-moral levels (*bricolage*). Individuals in the process of forming intentions are *bricoleurs*. They are juggling a multiplicity of attitudes, ideas, concepts, motives, beliefs in their attempt to form a particular intention.

Derrida's system is basically a system which is no system. Intention will emerge formed from and by the very multiplicity. Multiplicity is approached from what he calls a "natural attitude"[8] which observes the freeplay of the mul-

---

[6] Thiemann, 495.

[7] Jack Goody, *The Domestication of the Savage Mind*, (Cambridge University Press, 1977), 40, 144, 146. See also Claude Levi-Strauss in the bibliography for a more full treatment of the concept of *bricolage*.

[8] Derrida, *Writing and Difference*, (The University of Chicago Press, 1978), 144.

tiplicity and in the freeplay, differences are noted and as the multiple differences accumulate, the natural attitude constructs them into a particular system or form and Derrida suggests that as soon as this construction is done, a deconstruction quite naturally begins which throws the system into a freeplay of multiple difference again. Derrida feels that the construction, deconstruction and reconstruction cycle of freeplay of differences is itself a rupturous, violent series of events to both the constructor and the construction. But the need to construct, deconstruct and reconstruct and otherwise systematise in new, better, more efficient ways, is again the Niagara tendency of the mind seeking the blessed rage for order, indeed needing, oneness in the multiplicity. Derrida calls this oneness an imagined force at a centre which gives meaning to the whole, the chaos and multiplicity. However, as soon as an apparent force or centre is discovered, systematised, located, it is deconstructed by the natural freeplay of its own differences.

Now Derrida applied this mostly to written texts, as I said earlier, literature, that can be deconstructed and reconstructed as a freeplay of differences. But in terms of religious life, catholicity, church dogma, morality, and intention formation, this simply means that we too are engaged in a freeplay of difference with regard to our intentions, the development and interpretation of dogma, church history, morality and especially scripture. In conversations as church, at whatever level, people are engaged in this freeplay of difference but often become quite frightened when the freeplay becomes systematised in a particular way, such that they might have an infallible proclamation from the pope on faith or morals or vice versa, they might be equally scared to live continually in a chaotic freeplay.

The very proclamation of the *de fide* doctrine of infallibility is just such a one. Once this proclaiming is done, it really doesn't leave much room for discussion, like the Ayatollah's *fatwa* on Salmon Rushdie. In fact, when people ask me about the doctrines of the Assumption or Infallibility, I respond, I think, as any layperson might, not having studied Hans Kung or the history of the development of the doctrine of infallibility in any detail, that there's really not much to say about them except to leave them stand as the structures they are— frozen in time and really not impacting much of anything because the church hierarchy insists that they remain frozen constructs. Further, why would I even set about to deconstruct the doctrine of the Assumption? What would be my motive? I more likely would deconstruct the language that the dogma is written in.

An attendant fellow whom I'd like to mention in connection with Derrida is the German theologian Rudolf Bultmann. He introduced this wonderfully radical idea of deconstruction into the arena of theology and religion, most particularly in his focus on demythologizing, which is a form of deconstruction on a different level. Religions tend to form these hard and fast, immutable constructs, and Derridean philosophy opens the possibility of reconstruction, rereading, re-interpreting the myths of religions. Bultmann, and others after him, point out that there are certain truths and facts that people hold dear about God and Jesus and religious life and practices, but these myths need to be remythologised. The key to remember about the myth is that there is a kernel of truth, a core, a center which Derrida would of course reconstruct but Bultmann says that in many cases the truth or kernel has been so buried by cumulative interpretations and re-tellings that it is lost and may have to be demythologised and remythologised. Through scripture studies and the disciplines of archaeology and paleontology, work is being done in this area. The late Joseph Campbell also did some significant work in this area with his book on *The Power of Myth*.

Like Derrida's *differance* or Ong's constructive relationality, or Lonergan's recognition of the fact of multiplicity in historical record, Rudolf Bultmann has his concept of "demythologising" with regard to the reading and interpretation of scripture.

> This method of interpretation of the New Testament which tries to recover the deeper meaning behind the mythological conceptions I call de-mythologizing—an unsatisfactory word, to be sure. Its aim is not to eliminate the mythological statements, but to interpret them. It is a method of hermeneutics. . . . a method of interpretation . . . the art of exegesis.[9]

Bultmann goes on to discuss that this demythologising began in the New Testament itself with Paul and John. Jewish apocalyptic expectations of a Mes-

[9] Rudolf Bultmann, *Jesus Christ and Mythology*, (New York: Charles Scribner's Sons), pp. 18, 45.

sianic Kingdom became for Paul a Messianic interregnum where the Messiah did come, left, and the return is awaited. However, for John, the coming of the Messiah and his departure and return are all within the same continuum of eternity, and also within the Jewish expectation (33-35).

This task of demythologising (like Derrida's deconstruction) has "no other purpose but to make clear the call of the Word of God." It interprets, seeks meaning, and frees the Word from the constrictions of time and space. Bultmann defends it not as a mere rationalising or as a way of reducing scripture to a mere human product, but rather as a means of making clear the incomprehensibility of the mystery of God as something beyond human theoretical thought.

Hans Urs von Balthasar's *Truth is Symphonic: Aspects of Christian Pluralism* sets forth another wonderful image for plurality and unity in the symphony. There is indeed one truth, one God, one dogma, one absolute good, but it is symphonic, a multiple blend of a variety of voices. The paradox, the contradiction then arises that when we take the one truth, the one good, apart, we find a multiplicity of discordant voices and instruments which, when separate, are quite interesting; once they begin to play together, however, there may be, indeed will be, a discord, disharmony, tuning as they work toward symphony wherein each will still retain its discordant, disharmonious difference but in symphony with other differences. The discord is not really perceived nor can the symphony perceive the discord: that is the paradox. Von Balthasar makes the important point that when we are confronted with mystery, the only way, the one way, to consider it is from the perspective of constant contrast, discord and difference; an inexhaustible, unexpected multiplicity and plurality. If, he says, in our elucidation of mystery, some aspects become very clear and lucid from a rational point of view, then we have probably lost hold of the mystery.[10] Mystery means a constant juggling of differences, interplay of rational, lucid points of view; a constant deconstruction and reconstruction of differences.

---

[10] Hans Urs von Balthasar, *Truth is Symphonic: Aspects of Christian Pluralism*, trans. by Graham Harrison, (San Francisco: Ignatius Press, 1987), 65.

Von Balthasar also raises an interesting point which Derrida addresses—and that is the interplay between absence and presence.[11] In other words, a particular construction, by its very nature, assumes the presence of the absence of another construction, reminiscent of the old philosophical conundrum that defines good as the absence of evil and vice versa. As we discern differences and attempt to construct unified systems from the pluralities, we necessarily create absences. "If I am this, then I am not that." Von Balthasar makes the interesting point that in plurality we can expect the unexpected. Sometimes something is present in its absence—like God. Von Balthasar says that essentially God is revealed in multiple, unexpected ways; God is present in the discernment of difference, but God is still as yet, always already, absent.[12] Derrida develops the paradox in great detail and basically says that if someone or something, some idea or system or construct or intention is present, visible, known, this necessarily affirms the absence of another equally viable construction, making what was absent present and what was present absent. Derrida has this wonderful phrase running through his many volumes "the always already absent present of a chain of signifiers."[13] The phrase assumes a certain timelessness, placelessness—like the Psalm says "for God 1000 years are as a day and a day as a thousand years." Something, someone, some idea or system or intention is always already present as it is signified in word or action or whatever the structure; while, on the other hand, some other something, someone, idea or system or intention is always already absent because it is not signified in any particular word, action or system; it needs to be constructed, thereby displacing the first construction—a chain of intentions.

Consciousness of difference is the basis of unity. Conflict, an active consequence of difference, is the obverse, the inverse, the other side of the coin, of commonality. The fear is that if there is conflict, argument and difference, then community and unity are lost. However, the fear is equally strong that where

---

[11] Gayatri Spivak, "Translator's Preface," to *Of Grammatology*, (Baltimore: The Johns Hopkins University Press, 1974), xvii.

[12] Spivak, xix, xxi.

[13] Jacques Derrida, *Of Grammatology*, trans. Gayatri Chakravorty Spivak, (Baltimore: The Johns Hopkins University Press, 1974), 157, 311.

there is apparent commonality and unity, no conflict, no tensions, no disagreement, that community appears as a group of robots mechanically performing tasks in the name of unity.

Leonardo Boff in his article "Trinitarian Community and Social Liberation" discusses the roots of the Greek word *koinonia*, a word that has come to us meaning or suggesting a community of people who serve each other out of love[14] but Raimundo Pannikar points out that the word is also derived from a Greek word *koinou* which means "impure"[15] and he suggests by this that the impurity in the community of services is its multiplicity, its diversity. Anselm Min in his article "The Challenge of Radical Pluralism" writes that radical pluralism means a constant, permanent, unrelenting process of active reciprocity[16]—a mutual acceptance of constant ongoing difference and distinction. As Cardinal Newman writes "To live is to change and to be perfect[ed] is to have changed often."[17] Radical pluralism means confronting systems with a final, irreducible otherness which reduces the system's assertion of itself to silence, solitude and re-evaluation. When one intention is formed, it will preclude the inclusion of other intentions. The key task in radical pluralism is the right and activity of self-definition, self-description and self-understanding and a reconstruction of these—the recognition of one's own limits as they impact upon each other and others. Pannikar writes that Christianity by *its own* self-definition actually says that it stands ready to accept any culture, language or tradition.[18] Pannikar makes the provocative point that just as Christianity declared at its first Council of Jerusalem described in the *Acts of the Apostles* that circumcision is not necessary to become a Christian—anyone is welcome—

---

[14] Leonardo Boff, "Trinitarian Community and Social Liberation," (*Cross Currents*, Volume 38, #3, 1988), 299.

[15] Raimundo Pannikar, "Chosenness and Universality: Can Christians Claim Both?" (*Cross Currents*, Volume 38, #3, 1988), 312.

[16] Anselm Min, "The Challenge of Radical Pluralism," (*Cross Currents*, Volume 38, #3, 1988), 272-3.

[17] John Henry Cardinal Newman, *An Essay on the Development of Christian Doctrine*, (University of Notre Dame Press, 1989), 40.

[18] Pannikar, 323.

maybe there should be a Council of Jerusalem II which says baptism is not necessary[19]—Christianity embraces any culture, language, tradition—this is an essential part of Christianity's self-definition—that it embraces difference, the radical plurality and otherness of whoever comes. Christianity does not reduce the radical otherness and plurality by insisting on a mechanical, exterior community which masks difference.

Roman Catholics might, for example, ask the pope and Curia in Rome to please be attentive to and hear their differences. Please hear the ways in which others in the world experience God which may be radically alien to their personal experiences in Rome and then trust those ways and experiences that others have revealed and care for their difference, nurture them and trust their voices, their differences; they will return trust to their leader and bridge builder between all these different experiences and perceptions of God.[20] Specifically, in our time, we are invited to hear the voices not only of other cultures and religions but simply of our women, married, single, religious, who offer possibly the greatest single potential for re-creation, re-construction, re-perception of multiplicity and plurality in the church in the rather complicated task of deconstructing the patriarchal structure and reconstructing it to include women as leaders.

Father Ong, the linguist and literary scholar whom I mentioned earlier, uses the parable of the yeast (Matthew 13:33) as an analogue or figure for multiplicity and understanding pluralism. In his article, "Realizing Catholicism: Faith, Learning and the Future," his metaphor simply asserts that just as the end product cannot be observed in the small mustard seed or the yeast, so too the end product of unity, catholicity, community or formed intention cannot be reached or seen unless the community, the person, proceeds through the seeds of plurality and difference. Father Ong writes that the limitlessness, the plurality of possibilities for growth and development and change is what gives the church, the community, its depth.[21] The illusion is that the community, the Roman Catholicity is weakened, the foundations are shaken by radical pluralism

---

[19] Pannikar, 324.

[20] James Roberts, "Priest's Plea to the Pope: Hear Us," (*The Province*, September 16, 1984), 29.

[21] Ong, 334.

128

and division and dissent, but in truth, or perhaps just another construct, another illusion created as we proceed on our way, is that there is a paradox here, an apparent contradiction, like the death-resurrection, the disharmonious harmony of the symphony. Illusion-reality, fact-fiction binaries—an apparent aberrant, rampant, chaotic pluralism is actually the bedrock for unity, the signifiers of community. The more pluralism and difference, the more community, the more intentions.

Another of Father Ong's assertions I would like to attend to briefly on my way to a conclusion is that he takes the discussion of plurality and unity to a level of the individual person, the "I."[22] The multiplicity, the plurality present there is held together by the unifying pronoun "I." There is no "I" without a multiplicity of selves who exist at various times and places and comprise the "I." There is no "we" as community of church without the multiplicity of our "I's." The multiplicity in a text needs to be given voice so that its unity as text can be experienced. This microcosm of multiplicity in united text is another analogue, another metaphor for the microcosm of a multiple, plural group of persons in a united government, state, church, family. And this multiplicity of "I's," this plurality of selves in collegial conversation about ideas, concepts, feeling, beliefs, is a process through which intentions are formed.

I will conclude this chapter on religious pluralism with Thomas Merton, the sixties monk and activist. He has one significant story which interestingly was in his last speech given in Bangkok, Thailand on December 10, 1968, in which he tells his audience that structures will fail. He then paused to emphasise very carefully that if they remember anything of what he said, it is this that "from now on everybody stands on his own two feet."[23] Whatever happens, whatever structures do in fact collapse and disappear, the true, unavoidable fact of the matter is that each of us must stand alone, on our own two feet, without those structures as structures in ourselves who form intentions. If we look at Merton himself as a structure on which people depended and depend, it is even more interesting that he concludes his lecture on that day by saying "well, I

---

[22] Ong, 334.

[23] Thomas Merton, "Marxism and Monastic Perspectives," Appendix VII of *The Asian Journal of Thomas Merton*, (New York: New Directions Publishing Corporation, 1973), 338.

guess the plan is for you to have a discussion later this evening about the various presentations so I will disappear." He does indeed disappear; he dies. But what he implies is that he deconstructs himself as a system; he deconstructs his own presentation and hands it over to the participants who will each construct according to their own lights—they will each stand on their own two feet and construct as they wish and they will disappear. But in terms of religion, theology and morality, intention formation, this activity is done in faith.

> I am only 52 years old and like every other Christian I am occupied in the great affair of saving my sinful soul in which grace and psychology are sometimes in rather intense conflict. I am certainly aware of the fact that my life is not necessarily a history of fidelity to grace and like every other Christian I can only admit my failures and beg the Lord to have mercy on me. If in trying to give thanks to God for His mercies, I have sometimes helped others, I am glad. But I still need the prayer and the compassion of my fellow Christians . . . .[24]

> . . . that which is most perfect and most individual in each [person's] life is precisely the element in it which cannot be reduced to a common formula. It is the element which is nobody else's but ours and God's. It is our own, true, incommunicable life, the life that has been planned for us and realized for us in the bosom of God.[25]

Just as there is a multiplicity in texts and in persons, there is also multiplicity in theology and morality, in religion and church. A formation of intention about dogmatic interpretation is constituted in the multiplicity, almost bordering on chaos, evidenced in the bible and in history. The task of the interpreter or of one who is forming structures and/or intentions, is to use the tools of hermenuetics (demythologising, deconstructing) such that entities which "stand on their own two feet" may converse and exchange in a constructive

---

[24] Michael Mott, *The Seven Mountains of Thomas Merton*, (Boston: Houghton Mifflin Company, 1984,) xxvi. This quote is from an unpublished January 7, 1967 letter to a student who was writing a thesis on Merton and wanted to include a long biographical section.

[25] Thomas Merton, *The Sign of Jonas*, (New York: Harcourt, Brace and Company, 1953), 181.

relationality, an active reciprocity, still respecting the mystery of each entity, each interpretation, each conversation. In the next and final chapter, I will revisit and re-interpret Wimsatt and Beardsley's intentional and affective fallacies in the light of my remarks about how intention and affect are formed and I conclude that *a text* can have its own intention and affect as formed by the language, the rhetoric there, apart from the reader and author. All these are the work of the same Spirit who distributes different gifts to different people.

"It's no use blaming the mirror if your face is crooked."

—A Russian proverb used by
Nikolai Gogol in 1835 as an epigraph to
his play *The Inspector General.*

CONCLUSION

The Intentional and Affective Fallacies Revisited

Nothing that goes into someone from outside can make that person unclean; it is the things that come out of someone that make the person unclean . . . .

Mark 7: 15

I have attempted in this book to elaborate and concretise in prose and with examples from various academic disciplines my ongoing fascination with a formation of intention process. Basically, my belief is that words, behaviours and thoughts, exterior and interior lives, are mirrors of each other or parts of each other at a variety of levels. A part of one word, behaviour or thought can constitute a part of another word, behaviour or thought. A part of one can "perform" (in the sense of "be a performative") for another. I have looked in detail at the various ways that this reciprocity or mirroring can occur, and I have attempted to put into language, a rhetoric, a coming to terms, a naming, of these intersections and their various matrices.

Edmund Husserl's phenomenology, Plato's metaphysics, and Derrida's deconstruction theory clarify in terms of the discipline of philosophy the interlace of desire, intentionality, motivation, and attitude which science or medicine may speak of as neurochemistry or biochemistry. When the neurochemical, interior gestalt is articulated, then a mirror is created. Does the articulation, the languaging, the rhetoric, if you will, truly represent, imitate, the interior or exterior reality, depending on the case? Is the naming of the neurochemical reactions, the electrical impulses in the brain, as "desire," "thought," "attitude," "motive," an effective, helpful terminology? When the neurochemical, interior gestalt is mirrored again in words or behaviours, first of all, does the particular word or behaviour indeed mirror the interior reality, the interior experience, and if so, is it only part of that interior experience and what part and how is it related to the whole? Is it constituted there or does the external behaviour or word return to the person and constitute the interior neurochemistry?

When literature and art approach this problematic, I feel that they provide a clarity that other disciplines do not in the sense that literature is a universal language, has a universal appeal, is a "rhetoric" that is accessible, hence my selection of works by Chaucer, DeQuincey, Fielding, and Greene. Similar analyses of dramatic works (perhaps those by Edward Albee and Tennessee Williams) would require a slightly different approach, since "imitation" or representation is acted out, occurs before the eyes and ears of viewers, like film, and other levels come into play. Theological and religious pluralism exemplify multiplicity in their search for dogmatic unity and catholicity when they arrive at any unity or concensus. They realise that if they hold the mirror back on the process, a multiplicity and plurality will be mirrored back.

The terminology of speech act theory also helped me to elaborate and support my beliefs, and the question of "referentiality" in language is key, since references occur and interlace at all three levels of word, behaviour and thought in various mathematical permutations and computations. Simply put, realities are named with language or behaviour and the question arises whether the language, the terminology, accurately refers to the reality being named or is the languaging itself the reality to which the behaviour refers? In terms of grammar, this is the perennial problem of antecedent and pronoun reference. When words like "he or she" are used in English, do they refer to someone, and if so to whom? Similarly, when a behaviour occurs can it be accurately named and referred to; is the language of history, for example, effective in doing this?

Transformational grammar places "word" in writing rather than orality (speech), and its terminology of deep and surface structures again supports my point about varieties of levels. However, I do not care for the spatial terms "deep" and "surface," I prefer to differentiate them by simply calling them "another structure." Chomsky looks at a particular sentence and takes the traditional tool of diagramming (parsing), but does so with the intention of having the surface structure of the diagram refer to a deeper structure, an "innate language" in all persons regardless of native language from which arises a language that is unique to that particular person and which that particular person must translate into the language of his or her particular culture and nation.

I believe that a "rhetoric" of a formation of intention is helpful to people who simply want to separate and re-mix their so-called illusions from their realities, accidents from substances, trivialities from essentials, performatives, and constatives, and I believe that this rhetoric can be interdisciplinary.

In arguing for a "rhetoric" for a formation of intention, I maintain that such a rhetoric and such formation and intentionality must be located only in and from the object itself: text, author, reader. In other words, when I read a particular written text, it can have an intentional-rhetorical-affective structure in and of itself separate from author and reader. This is basically Wimsatt and Beardsley's argument in their articles on the intentional and affective fallacies which I shall now address.

In 1946, W.K. Wimsatt and Monroe Beardsley set forth their intentional/affective fallacy theories. Their point is that a work of art stands quite separately from the artist's intention and an individual person's emotional responses to the art. They argue that authorial design and intention are neither available nor desirable, and are probably inaccessible. I wish to add to their argument by saying that the work of art itself, notably a piece of literature, has an intentional-affective structure of its own accessible through its own language and structure. Whether the author intended this structure or not is secondary. Intentional structure can be accessed in the text and the characters represented there. A text may portray a particular character who has a particular structure which I have illustrated in a previous chapter.

Up to this point, I have demonstrated the intentional structure of particular characters in particular works. The authors structured the characters such that an intentional structure emerges evidenced in the particular character's words and behaviours: the Troilus and Criseyde relationship, the "unfortunate gilt" of Leonora in *Joseph Andrews*, the Graham Greene affair, and Thomas DeQuincey's exit from Manchester. Dogmatic/moral structures in religious settings have an intentional–affective content in their texts. A particular dogmatic construct or moral imperative can be deconstructed for intention and affect.

But now, by way of conclusion, I wish to look at a dramatic work itself, by way of Wimsatt and Beardsley's articles, rather than a character or author, and discuss *its* intention and design as an external object. The difference is that the words on the page can't *do* anything; they are their own behaviour. The language itself expresses intention and affection quite apart from reader interpretation or authorial affect and intention. The words may quite simply, apparently, spring from the author onto the page and then spring from there to the reader and they, the words on the page, become a "thing," an object in their (its) own right. How they affect readers emotionally, interpretively, is another, different process again that springs from the particular reader/critic.

Samuel Beckett, like many authors and artists, was concerned about this with regard to his own work. He has said that the texts of his plays are to stand as something quite separate from him. When he directed or worked on one of his own plays, he might change something but he still maintained that the original stood as it was originally written and that such changes create a new piece, a different version. If the change was his, the change is still under the purview of the author; however, if done by a director, the change can in effect create an entirely new piece. Actors or directors of a Beckett piece must be very careful to keep their own affective-intentional materials separate from the work; they must attempt to decipher as closely as possible their intentional-affective structure of the particular piece, a formidable task for any Beckett play. His trustees recently disclaimed any connection with a version of *Waiting for Godot* which was to use 5 women. Beckett's text indicates that the play is to be acted by men and to change the characters to women would radically alter the text's intentional structure, and in this case, via Beckett's trustees, *his* intentional structure. The many references to prostate-urinary difficulties in the play themselves compound the gender problem.

Beckett also disclaimed any connection with a production of his newly-written, 40 second piece called *Breath* where the director had placed among the "miscellaneous, vertical garbage" some nude bodies. This was not part of the intentional structure of the text for the piece nor Beckett's intentional structure as author.

To cut the spontaneous combustion of the parasol sequence (for all its theatrical difficulty) in *Happy Days* seriously mars the intentional structure of the piece. With Beckett's plays, the cast and crew and director need to spend a good deal of their initial work in deciphering the intentional-affective structure of the particular piece they are working on by first looking carefully at the words in the text itself and then possibly comments by Beckett himself about the work. But these are two different affective-intentional structures: that of Beckett and of his particular piece. The affective-intentional structure of the characters in the piece might be addressed along with the overall development of plot and thematic progression of images, etc. The actual language of the piece on the pages of the text needs to be read with great care.

The character of Willie in *Happy Days* is interesting and problematic simply because there is so little to work with. He says and does very little in the piece. His intentional-affective structure is fairly inaccessible. So the actor must be careful not to superimpose motives and intentions. If Willie's motives and intentions are inaccessible, or at least questionable, then the actor playing Willie simply speaks the lines as written and executes the movements written. Willie moves in and out of his hole and reads various employment notices from Reynolds' newspaper, covers his head, apparently to protect himself from the blazing, hot desert-like sun, and answers a few of Winnie's questions, notably in one case with a simple, stark "yes." He hums "The Merry Widow" waltz and at the end moves around to the other side of the mound in which his wife, Winnie, is buried, and both she and the audience (and possibly the director and actor) wonder what he is doing. When he attempts to climb the mound toward Winnie and utters her name, abbreviated to "Win," in a barely audible tone, has he lost his mind? Has he gone deaf and dumb? His intentional-affective structure is not accessible and so he must be played that way by the actor. Interpretations seem to multiply exponentially and create more confusion than clarity about this character. If the actor or director superimposes a particular intention or emotion, they may be doing something to Willie that is not there, giving him an intentional-affective structure that the text does not indicate that he has. Why is he "dressed to kill" for example at the end of the play? Where did he get the clothes? When does he change? Does he change more than his clothes? Is he going for the gun to kill Winnie? She doesn't know. Nor do we. Beckett never indicated. Part of the Willie written into this text is a Willie who "doesn't know" and if he does, he's not telling what he knows, intends or feels and his behaviour is unclear. The actor must portray this ambiguity, this confusion.

Wimsatt and Beardsley argue that the "design or intention of the author is neither available nor desirable as a standard for judging the success of a work of literary art."[1] They are aware that they are divorcing such difficult problems as authorial inspiration, textual authenticity rooted in the author, and biographical impacts. The work of art is judged separately from its author and hence so is the intentional-affective structure of each. Certainly the work finds inspiration, source and authenticity in an author but the intentional-motivational-emotional structures may be quite different. Graham Greene made a similar point when he asserted that he was a writer who happened to be Catholic, not a Catholic writer. In other words, his personal, biographical life included the Catholic religion and his novels included reference to the Catholic religion and Catholic moral problems specifically, but he maintained that the one did not come from or refer to the other. His being Catholic was quite different from his novels being Catholic. He became quite distressed after writing *The Heart of the Matter*, not only because it was put on the Index of Forbidden books by Rome but also because people were calling him to be their spiritual director.

Margaret Atwood has done the same thing in recent interviews about her work. She singlemindedly succeeds in keeping herself separate from her work when interviewers attempt to locate her particular demons in her intentional-affective structure that would produce the dystopic intentional-motivational structure of *The Handmaid's Tale*, for example. There is a difference between source, authenticity and authorial inspiration for a text and the intentional-motivational-affective structure of the text itself and the characters in the text. Many authors will say that they don't know where particular characters came from nor how they developed. The characters just sort of took on a life of their own, using the author's talent and imagination as their vehicles to come into being.

---

[1] W.K. Wimsatt and Monroe C. Beardsley, "The Intentional Fallacy," in *Critical Theory Since Plato*, edited by Hazard Adams, (New York: Harcourt, Brace, Jovanovich, Inc., 1971), p. 1015.

It is not necessary that readers know what an author intended. The author may not even know. However, it is necessary to know that the work is rooted in a particular person's inspiration, a particular person's affective-intentional structure which has a biographical history all its own. Authors become characters in their own autobiographies or they become characters in the texts of other authors known as biographers. In point of fact, the text may have a radically different, however complementary, affective-intentional structure and may spark a chain of inspiration elsewhere. The author's intentional-affective structure may indeed have an attitude toward the intentional-affective structure of the author's own textual creation.

Wimsatt and Beardsley make the key point that structural "design" of a text certainly does come from an author but should not be the standard of judgement nor should the structural effects that occur in readers. The concern needs to switch from "what the author intended or tried to do" to "what does the text in fact do and intend and affect." In other words, a reader could say to the author, "your text seems to intend this or affect that, would you agree? How do you read your own text as author?" The author may respond by saying "is that an affect or an intention that you see as reader? I, as author, don't *see* those but now that you say them, I can see them there in my own text." What the intentional-affective fallacies highlight and juxtapose is the traditional author-text-reader triangle in different ways, using different foci, different rhetorics from theorists like Wolfgang Iser or Roman Jakobson. Rather than talking about an overlap of affect and intention in text-reader-author, I am asserting that they each can and usually do have a very different affective-intentional structure which are in conversation and interpretation with and of each other. The text interprets the reader just as much as the reader interprets the text. If the reader has the privilege of authorial presence, there may be a three-way conversation and interpretation. The fact of the matter is that when a text "works" for readers, as Wimsatt and Beardsley write, it is natural for readers to "infer intention in the artificer." It would be equally appropriate and feasible to infer intention in the artifact.

Wimsatt and Beardsley use the genre "poetry" as the text or work of art and they concede that a text or work of art, like a poem, can be said to have a "personality or state of soul"(p. 1015) and thoughts and attitudes need to be at-

138

tributed to speakers there in the text and to the author only in biographical reference and correlation. The thoughts and attitudes of the author and/or reader can
and do interact with the text and with the author, revision and re-write can occur
and with the reader, new texts could be written.

But what the author intends could still be quite different from what the
text intends and the author's revision could be to clarify textual intentional structure, not authorial, and certainly not the reader's intentional-affective structure.
Wimsatt and Beardsley differentiate reader from critic. If a reader is a critic,
authorial intention and motivation will be brought into question,

> The poem [text] is not the critic's [reader's] own and not the
> author's (it is detached from the author at birth and goes
> about the world beyond his power to intend about it or con-
> trol it). The poem belongs to the public. It is embodied in
> language, the peculiar possession of the public and it is about
> the human being, an object of public knowledge.   (p. 1016)

Wimsatt and Beardsley refer to a criticism by Ananda Coomaraswamy
(p. 1016) about an artist achieving his intention and whether the work should
have been undertaken at all and is worth preserving or being preserved in the
canon, and they argue that these are moral/artistic questions generally. Only the
artist can say to what extent intention, aim, or goal was achieved in a particular
text, and whether it is worth preserving is determined by its popularity,
saleability and the degree of response it receives. Whether it should or should
not have been undertaken is truly a moral question that rests with the artist.

Wimsatt and Beardsley refer to Longinus' reference that Homer entered
into the sublime action of his own heroes. Homer, as author, related to his text and
its characters as something other. Homer becomes reader/critic of his own text
and may re-write and revise it, at which point he returns to it as author. But the
fact that he enters into the sublimity of his own text separates the two. Questions
about authorial intention, purpose and goal, reasonability and success of "plan"
are essentially auto/biographical questions. Wimsatt and Beardsley call on Plato,

> I went to the poets . . . I took them some of the most
> elaborate passages of their own writings and asked what was
> the meaning of them . . . there is hardly a person present

who would not have talked better about their poetry than they did themselves. Then I knew that not by wisdom do poets write but by a sort of genius or inspiration. (p. 1017)

This genius and inspiration are separate considerations from affect and intention. The text arises from the author as naturally as leaves on a tree. The text is the lava of imagination or as Beckett says in the negative, the excrement of his mind, the result of emotion (affect) recollected in tranquillity. Housman on the poetic mind:

> Having drunk a pint of beer at luncheon . . . I would go for a walk for 2-3 hours. As I went along, thinking of nothing in particular, only looking at things around me and following the progress of the seasons, there would flow into my mind with sudden unaccountable emotion, sometimes a line or two of verse, sometimes a whole stanza at once. (p. 1017)

Here the nature walk is the text for Housman who then writes a poem and the reader walks through the nature of that text with a similar "thinking nothing in particular," an openness.

Wimsatt and Beardsley maintain that an author is moved and persuaded by any number of layers and degrees of intentional-motivational-affective interstices to write a particular text, and if that text causes motive-intention-affect to arise in the reader, they are two quite separate movements and the tones in the text may be separate again. If authors, readers and critics are true to themselves, honest with themselves, know and reverence themselves, they will be similarly reverential, honest and true with the text. The degrees of truth, honesty, emotion, knowledge are fine-grained in all three.

Both author and reader (critic), with Housman, drink, relax, walk, look, surrender, search, listen, discover, express. Varieties of kinds of texts will emerge. Wimsatt and Beardsley's articles are rich in intertext themselves. They move from critic to critic in support of their argument. Criticism and judgment of text is quite different from simply reading them and different again from writing them. Psychological, auto/biographical curiosity about the genesis of a text is another aesthetic. Questions about authorial sincerity, spontaneity, fidelity, originality, authenticity are radically different from questions about textual integrity, relevance, unity, function and subtlety, and again different from the aesthetic of reader response which is again objectification of reader feeling and structure. The text itself is quite clearly an objectification because I have it there in front of me, but authorial and readerly intention and affect are not so clearly objectified. The activity of the critic might more appropriately be to re-construct the text in such a way that the reconstruction explicates an inherent affective-intentional structure in the text. Similarly, the activity of the biographer reconstructs the life of a person in a text and explicates an intentional-affective structure in the person. Readers may re-construct their own affective-intentional structures in a text, through a text, by a text, but based on the reading of other texts: an author's auto/biographies or novels or the historical development of texts, their reversions and revisions.

Wimsatt and Beardsley then make a point of the rhetoric of the text: grammar, syntax, idiosyncratic structures, linguistics; the surface structures and deep structures of the text, it's external and internal workings similar to what Barthes did with *Sarasine* in *S/Z*.

As I have indicated in earlier chapters, my thesis here is heavily informed and influenced by deconstruction theory: texts, authors and readers (critics) not only intersect with each other but interact within each other: texts, authors and readers (critics) have their own "histories" which converse and deconstruct among each other: "clusters of complex relations." Wimsatt and Beardsley assert a syntheses from the streamy nature of associations, combinations and permutations that constantly re-arrange, like atoms, alive, dynamic, moving.

However, the problem with objectification of text is that it indeed does become severed from roots, from author. Texts remain alive in their interactions with other texts which is done by readers, critics and authors. Critical texts of Plato, Longinus, Coleridge and Arnold are kept alive here in Wimsatt and Beardsley texts, and I keep Wimsatt and Beardsley alive in mine here.

Wimsatt and Beardsley exemplify their theory briefly and concisely with a quatrain from John Donne's "Valediction Forbidding Mourning" followed by one paragraph of critical commentary of Charles Coffin, followed by their own deconstruction of Coffin, who they say is setting Donne's quatrain in the single context of the new science of his age. The intertexts are Kepler's *De Stella*

Nova, Galileo's *Siderius Nuncius*, Gilbert's *De Magnate* etc. which they assume Donne has read since beside "Valediction," other of his poems indicate a resonance around this constellation of theological problems of minister Donne and his century's new science. However, Wimsatt and Beardsley do not wish to make the geocentric/heliocentric antithesis the core metaphor for Donne's work and they set about to do a minor four point deconstruction which I will not elaborate here since I have, I believe, clearly made my point about the gestalt of authors, readers, critics and texts and their interstices. (see Part IV [pp. 1018 ff] of their article "The Intentional Fallacy.")

Another word for intertext might be the literary device called allusion as used by T.S. Eliot. Wimsatt and Beardsley write that some texts like "The Waste Land" can really only be understood if one has read other texts, if one can recognise the allusions in "The Waste Land." They also suggest that the text gives insight into what Eliot has read in his life. Intentional-motivational-affective structure in a text can be determined by studying and structuring the allusions, the intertexts. Charles Gontarski has done this with Beckett's *Happy Days* where he uncovers a rich texture of hidden allusions there. Such structuring gives the text its own integrity, its own intentional-affective structure. However, obviously such allusiveness and extended connective links to other texts from other historical periods may actually make the text accessible only to the most educated, widely read. Footnoting allusions, as Eliot does, may only serve to complicate the structure unnecessarily, rather than clarify and simplify. Rather than ask what *Eliot* is doing here, the reader asks what the text is doing here with all the intertext, footnotes, allusions. Certainly Eliot, as author, might inform the reader about the text but in the name of the intentional-affective fallacies, these three need to remain as separate and objectified as possible. Proponents of authorial intention say that someone like Eliot did indeed have a plan or a structure he was executing in a particular poem. However, a reader or critic could re-structure the poem in such a way that it is not in keeping with Eliot's original plan (if indeed he had one). So the reader-critic constructs a parallel text for Eliot's plan. We have then three texts: the poem, Eliot's plan for the poem as he may explain it and the critic's plan. Wimsatt and Beardsley then proceed to a brief convergence of Eliot, Prufrock, Donne, Marvel where

Eliot, Donne and Marvel are intertexted as authors, and Prufrock is a character as text in a text.

Jonathan Culler in his *Structuralist Poetics* and Wolfgang Iser in *The Act of Reading* present two different understandings of the concept and process of combination, which I would like to address momentarily here. Culler explores various theorists and then decides to favour the term "network of relations"[2] as product-oriented, as opposed to the "changing of perspective" of the combination process. Iser says that combination is a reader process that involves a continuous interaction of texts with readers in varieties of constellations. Elements for him function as catalysts for other new chains of combinations. Iser sees such combinations as infinite. Every reading moment entails a possible switch in perspective, constituting a new set of differentiated combinations. The reader actively fills various gaps and blanks and blackholes in the text as the text may do for the reader. The reader creates these systems of combinations about a text in a coherent way, but the system and coherency can break down and be re-constructed. This constant changing of perspective for Iser is for Culler simply a series of limited sets of relationships. The danger with Culler's perspective is that the text does indeed become quite frozen and sterile, a verbal icon.

Stanley Cavell in a 1982 article "Politics as Opposed to What?" writes about the reader's active engagement with the text as an existential experience of Heidegger's "man thinking,"[3] actively engaging in combining and relating. There is a cognitive, active interaction. For Culler, the possible structures for texts are decided from outside readers while Iser and Cavell locate the infinite number of possibilities in the readers, the "reader thinking." Culler assumes that all readers could agree on a particular system of relations structure as a product, a systematisation of the text. Culler combines until a mutually agreed upon system is constructed. His process always has product in view, whereas Iser's process has itself as process in view, constant changing perspectives of reader thinking. Iser and Cavell encourage the reader to explore and combine freely according to their own interior logic. Such a process is lived, existential, engag-

---

[2] Jonathan Culler, *Structuralist Poetics: Structuralism, Linguistics and the Study of Literature,* (Ithaca, New York: Cornell University Press, 1975), pp. 10-16.

[3] Stanley Cavell, "Politics as Opposed to What?" *Critical Inquiry* (September, 1982), p. 174.

ing. Arriving at a product, a system for the text, certainly may happen, but it is not looked for, whereas Culler is constantly reading with a view to constructing this product, this system of relations. Culler would be pleased with author involvement; Iser would not. The reader should be free to examine texts without authorial intrusion. Iserian readers would approach texts and read them as they make sense of them. Cullerian readers would approach the same text, looking for its system, as something previously assumed, already there. Classics have come to be read this way. Canonical texts of Chaucer, Shakespeare, Milton have come down to readers and students with a superimposed combinatory, relational structure, like Culler proposes, however much they continued to be read, examined and studied. Some modern and post-modern texts of Beckett or Joyce or Virginia Woolf are more frustrating for Cullerian readers because as the reader reads, a system often does not form and the reader must become an Iserian combiner and structure the text according to personal lights and insights. For Culler, this is a combining problem but for Iser it is a combining pleasure, an activity. Barthes' *S/Z* is an Iserian reading.

Whereas the intentional fallacy confuses the text with its origins, its author, the affective fallacy confuses the texts with its results, its readers' interpretations and responses. Both are fallacious because they make the text relative to its author and/or reader. The truth is that the text can stand alone as an objective entity in itself.

In communion with other critical texts of their times, notably I.A. Richards, Wimsatt and Beardsley proceed to illustrate how the meaning or suggestiveness of a particular word or structure is indeed rooted in the author, since the author did the initial constructing, had the initial inspiration and will affect readers to various degrees as readers understand the words and meanings. However, aside from author-reader, the text has a structure. The words of the particular language and culture are arranged in sentence patterns composing the text, its rhetoric, its rhetorical stance, wherein may be found degrees of intentional-affective structuring. A word has an affective impact simply because that's the nature of the particular word. A sentence has a meaning to the extent that it has a goal in a particular context, and such intentions can be accessed in the structuring of the sentence itself and its context. However, access will involve interpretation and paraphrasing by readers. Semioticians would like to cre-

144

ate linguistic rules to stabilise response; a description or cognitive function of words. However, for the emotive function, there is no such rule. What a word suggests to readers can be as varied as the number of readers. This is the root of the problem of affective fallacy. The words and how they are structured in the text go beyond simply cognitive, objective description to the vague, shadowy, emotive meaning, suggestiveness, inference, import, feeling. Readers tend to say "my feeling or sense about this text is . . ." and here it is important to note that the reader's feeling or sense of the text is part of the reader's construct and if the reader wishes to locate that feeling or sense in the text, the reader is obliged to look quite specifically and closely at the text and demonstrate how particular words and sentences and structures go beyond their cognitive-descriptive clarity into this more vague, rhetorical realm of feeling or emotional suggestiveness. It is comparable to my earlier discussion of the internal trigger in the frog, the hand-raising, or the trip to Minnesota. With regard to intention, this is particularly problematic if intention is to be located in the text, found formed there:

> Such differentiation in vocabulary would have the merit of reflecting a profound difference in linguistic function—all the difference between grounds of emotion and emotions themselves, between what is immediately meant by words and what is evoked by the meaning of words or what more briefly might be said to be the import of the words themselves. (p. 1024)

A great deal of the emotive import and suggestiveness depends upon the descriptive-linguistic meaning and structure. Wimsatt and Beardsley give the example of "the General ordering an execution of" and "the General being guilty of the murder of . . ." (p. 1024) both descriptive-linguistic meanings have obviously different emotive import and suggestiveness about what the General is doing, which is the same action in both cases.

Winnie and Willie have this very problem in Beckett's *Happy Days*. Winnie very confidently proclaims "fear no more the heat of the sun"[4] and Wil-

---

[4] Samuel Beckett, *Happy Days* in the *Bedford Introduction to Drama* edited by Lee A. Jacobus (New York: St. Martin's Press, 1989), p. 813.

lie later says simply "fear no more" and she asks him "what? fear no more what?" But he simply, in an apparent frustration or impatience, screams "fear no more!" which sends Winnie rushing headlong back into her monologue, the basic text of the play. However, both the reader and/or the person acting the parts of Willie and Winnie wonder what Willie's words mean. With Winnie, our response may be "fear no more what? . . . the heat of the sun?" and Willie *seems* to be suggesting that Winnie simply stop fearing generally, not some particular object like the heat of the sun. A possible interpretation of her constant rush of words may be that they indicate she is filled with fear, and avoiding facing the fear with the words. Beckett, Ionesco, Albee, and the absurdists texts generally are replete with these words and sentences that cause the readers or interpreters to ask what they mean? What is implied? How do you read it? How did the writer intend and interpret it? It is these kinds of texts, the absurdists, the stream of consciousness writers, that are most valuable and have made their way into the canon simply because of the richness and variety of response. What a word or sentence or paragraph or text *does* to a person, a reader, is something *done in that person.* The text still stands on its own as an object causing emotional-intellectual reaction, which reactions Wimsatt and Beardsley remind us are often culturally based. What one culture will react to emotionally, another will not. Salmon Rushdie's book *Satanic Verses* is a most recent case in point.

Wimsatt and Beardsley caution that the realm of suggestiveness, inference, import, particularly the emotional reaction in the reader ventures not only into the area of the reader but into the complex field interrelations of culture, anthropology and affective psychology. Emotion can fortify intention and opinion, inflame motive. The descriptive, linguistic meaning in the text can be fortified and inflamed by suggestive, emotive words in combined contexts. In readers, however, and possibly in texts as well, a free-floating, inchoate range of emotional-cognitive materials converge and even border and enter the unconscious, the subconscious.

> The tourist who said a waterfall was pretty provoked the silent disgust of Coleridge, while the other who said it was sublime won his approval. This, as C.S. Lewis so well observes, was the same as if the tourist had said "I feel sick": and Coleridge thought "no, I feel quite well." (p. 1025)

Nick Dorochoff pointed out to me that the actual passage in C.S. Lewis' *The Abolition of Man* (pp. 14-15) is a panoply of intersecting interpretations.

> You remember that there were two tourists present: that one called it [the waterfall] "sublime" and the other "pretty:" and that Coleridge mentally endorsed the first judgment and rejected the second with disgust. Gaius and Titus comment as follows: [Now, Gaius and Titus are the fictional names that C.S. Lewis creates of the authors of a textbook for "boys and girls in the upper forms of schools." Lewis has nothing good to say about the book but he does not want "to pillory two modest practising school-masters who were doing the best they knew": but he can't keep silent so he proposes to conceal their real names as he critiques their book.] When the man said "that is sublime," he appeared to be making a remark about the waterfall. . . . Actually . . . he was not making a remark about the waterfall, but a remark about his own feelings. What he was saying was really "I have feelings associated in my mind, with the word "sublime," or shortly, "I have sublime feelings." Here are a good many questions settled in a pretty summary fashion. But the authors are not finished. They add: "This confusion is continually present in language as we use it. We appear to be saying something very important about something: and actually we are only saying something about our own feelings." The man who says this is sublime cannot mean "I have sublime feelings." Even if it were granted that such qualities as sublimity were simply and solely projected into things from our own emotions, yet the emotions which prompt the projection are the correlatives, and therefore almost opposites, of the qualities projected. The feelings which make a man call an object sublime are not sublime feelings but feelings of veneration. If "This is sublime" is to be reduced at all to a statement about the speaker's feelings, the proper translation would be "I have humble feelings." If the view held by Gaius and Titus were consistently applied it would lead to absurdities. It would force them to maintain that "you are contemptible" means "I have contemptible feelings:" in fact that "Your feelings are contemptible" means "my feelings are contemptible." But we need not

delay over this which is the very *pons asinorum* of our subject. It would be unjust to Gaius and Titus themselves to emphasize what was doubtless a mere inadvertence.

Coleridge uses the example of the two tourists to assert his own feelings that the waterfall is sublime, not pretty. He would be like a third tourist present who happens to agree with the second tourist's evaluation that the waterfall is sublime.

Gaius and Titus in their school textbook seem to be trying to teach, according to C.S. Lewis' reading, that this example of the waterfall is an example of how interpretations of texts are very often simply expressions of the interpreter's own feelings and thoughts rather than any expressions of truth about the text. According to Lewis' citations from Gaius and Titus, they seem to be saying that language can be confusing in the sense that we may sound like we are talking about some particular external object or text when actually we are talking about ourselves as objects or texts being interpreted.

Now, Lewis takes exception to this and says that Gaius and Titus are reducing the whole complexity of intertextual interpretations to an absurdity: my feelings are your feelings and vice versa. If I say "You are contemptible," I am really saying that "I am contemptible." He clarifies that an interpretive sentence like "I have sublime feelings" or "This is sublime" may simply indicate feelings of veneration and an interpretive sentence like "I have humble feelings" might be more accurate, a "proper translation."

Lewis' point, I think, is that interpretive exercises like this can be reduced to absurdity. Clearly, individuals vary in their interpretations of texts and objects. The fact that one tourist experiences the waterfall as sublime and the other experiences it as pretty are separated in two ways: the first is that neither interpretation may have anything to do with the speakers' feelings. Hence, secondly, Wimsatt and Beardsley's point is that individual interpretations and feelings are quite separate from the text (the affective fallacy—the text does not make the interpreter feel or think anything). And when they write that "this (Coleridge's waterfall tourists), as C.S. Lewis so well observes, was the same as if the tourist had said 'I feel sick:' and Coleridge thought 'no, I feel quite well,'" they are using C.S. Lewis' observation that this equation of feelings with texts is absurd. Also, feelings that emerge about a particular text can be as divergent and utterly unconnected as these sick and feeling well assertions. Saying that the waterfall (or any text or object) is pretty or sublime is the same as saying it makes me feel sick or it makes me feel well to the extent that the utterance of the observer or interpreter has nothing to do with the text itself. The utterance becomes a text for interpretation.

My point is that the text as object can have "feelings" or "thoughts" to the extent that these can be evidenced in the language of the text itself. A waterfall, as text, cannot really have "feelings" or "thoughts." It is simply an object in nature. Whereas a written text can express thoughts and feelings in language which can elicit thoughts and feelings in readers as interpreters and critics. But these are not equivalences. If I say that the waterfall is sublime and makes me feel humble and reverential and "quite well" and someone else says that the waterfall is pretty but gives feelings of sickness and disgust, then neither the waterfall, nor the two interpreters are "the same." They become three different objects or texts engaging in collaborative conversation. They are "the same" or "equal" in their difference. They are not equal in the sense that they are different. But they are equal in the sense that the difference in each needs to be respected. One is not hierarchised as better than another.

Wimsatt and Beardsley review other affective theories from Plato's "feeding and watering the passions" to Aristotle's catharsis and its modern analogues of "relief and sublimation," the "transport (sublime ectasis)" of Longinus and 18th century longinians, to the infection theory of Tolstoy, empathy of Lipps, related pleasure theories, relaxation theory of Penjon, laughter theory of Max Eastman. Seven of Ogden, Richards and Wood's sixteen types of aesthetic theory are affective, notably "synaesthesis (equilibrium of appetite)." (See Part III of "The Affective Fallacy.") The sincerity and intention of the critic-reader in affective theory parallels the sincerity and intention of the author in intentional theory. The problem with the affective theory may be summarised in such statements as Wimsatt and Beardsley point out:

> To read this book is like living through an experience rather
> than just reading about it . . . it (the text) means nothing to
> me unless it can carry me away with the gentle and pas-
> sionate pace of its emotion [affective fallacy—is it "its" emo-

tion or the reader's interpretation] over obstacles of reality into meadows and covers of illusion [the obstacles *are* the illusions] . . . the sole criterion for me as reader is whether the text can sweep me into emotion or illusion.   (p. 1026-7)

Wimsatt and Beardsley recall:

"All scientists," said D.H. Lawrence to Aldous Huxley "are liars . . . I don't care about evidence. Evidence doesn't mean anything to me. I don't feel it *here.*" And, reports Huxley, he pressed his two hands on his solar plexus.   (p. 1027)

Wimsatt and Beardsley further distinguish affective theory in terms of what and how readers say texts affect them in contradistinction to their investigation of how and what about texts affect other readers. They examine a whole range of psycho-physiological reactions evidenced in observable biochemical bodily changes. An emotion may be sincerely reported with no bodily reaction or change whatever, while bodily changes might be noted where no emotion is apparently felt. Longinus suggested that passions, emotions and such sublimities have their parallels not so much in bodily reactions as in the audacities and exaggerations, the rhetoric, the figures of speech used in the language. I.A. Richards further complicates and details the language problems by talking about the rhythm of the text, its form, wherein the location of meaning, affect or intention consists in multiple and inclusive constructs in the matrix or gestalt of the text. The purely affective in the reader (or text or author) remains quite subjective; concrete matter vanishes and the circle of investigation becomes too narrowed, too abstract. The affective and the intentional need to be considered together when investigating text, author, reader.

Exactitude in textual analysis, reader response, or authorial intention are not to be held up as essential at the expense of further imaginative work in all three. Textual analysis must awaken further analysis, further avenues of investigation. Reader affective reaction should awaken further affective-intentional combining and re-combining explorations. Location of authorial intentions and sources should serve to make the author more authentic as an imaginative creator of texts (not necessarily a text already produced since it has its own structure). Each text has its own subtle pattern of emotions which play at the level of disposition or attitude. There are degrees of disinterest, detachment, distance in each. Some authors wish to remain deliberately detached from their texts, as I have pointed out with regard to Margaret Atwood or Graham Greene. Some readers approach texts with a similar distance and often an elaborate, almost studied or postured disinterest, and many critics as readers cultivate this distance. Texts are distanced and/or detached by their language, their accessibility, their translatability of content, the complexities of figures, the audience addressed with its particular glossary. When readers of texts become critics (whether psychoanalytic, marxist, feminist, reader response, affective, intentional, sociological, deconstructionist, religious), they are again changing the matrix within themselves. The text itself is not necessarily marxist or intentional or feminist, the reader or critic is. Hence when the reader as literary critic becomes author and writes a text, then that critic's text becomes another intentional-affective object in itself with a particular critical matrix and structure.

How does a text "hold" ideas and emotions? Is it possible to look at a text and read it or talk about it as a living thing, a dynamic, moving, active organism with affective, intentional, factual content and structure? It is possible to the extent that it can be juggled, juxtaposed, re-arranged, re-combined, deconstructed and reconstructed. T.S. Eliot's "objective correlative" says that a text has idea and emotion that correlate to a logical chain within it. This of course is his personal theoretical reading as critic. Yvor Winters develops Eliot by saying that not only is there this objective correlative between emotion elicited and logical, qualitative progression of ideas and images in a text but also a surface texture or rhetorical structure that carry the elicitation and progression. Winters' reading is a re-versioning of Chomsky's transformational grammar which sees deep structure and meaning mirrored in the grammatical surface structure.

In this book, I have examined how language and rhetoric function in the formation of intentions and how formation of intentions is mirrored in the language and rhetoric of particular texts. I have done this by focusing on texts themselves as objects separate from their origins and/or ends. I have used various disciplines to assist me: pyschological and medical for individual persons as texts; philosophy through which I established a philosophy about what I am doing—specifically a philosophy of language, and speech act theory. Chomsky's transformational grammar and the tools of grammar generally have helped me focus on the mechanics of language, and the devices and plots of various pieces of literature have shown the mechanics of language in action. Finally, I have attempted to make the transition from the languages of literature and philosophy to theology and morality, where the use of language in formation of intention is most acute. And in conclusion, I have returned to the text as language object in my discussion of the affective-intentional fallacies. Again, I have attempted to show that formation of affect and intention resides in a text, as in characters and persons, quite apart from origins and ends.

For it is from within, from the heart, that evil intentions emerge. . . .

Mark 7: 21

LIST OF REFERENCES

Albee, Edward. *Who's Afraid of Virginia Woolf?* New York: Atheneum Press, 1975.

Anscombe, G.E.M. *Intention*. Ithaca: Cornell University Press, 1969.

Aquila, Richard E. *Intentionality: A Study of Mental Acts*. The Pennsylvania State University Press, 1977.

Austin, J.L. *How To Do Things With Words* Cambridge: Harvard University Press, 1962.

Van der Auwera, Johan. *Indirect Speech Acts Revisited*. Reproduced by the Indiana University Linguistics Club, 1980.

Bach, Kent and Robert M. Harnish. *Linguistic Communication and Speech Acts*. Cambridge, Massacheusetts: The MIT Press, 1979.

Baker, Lynne Rudder. *Saving Belief: A Critique of Physicalism*. Princeton University Press, 1987.

Ballmer, Th. and W. Brennenstuhl. *Speech Act Classification: A Study in the Lexical Analysis of English Speech Activity Verbs*. New York: Springer-Verglag, 1981.

Barfield, Owen. *Speaker's Meaning*. Middletown, Connecticut: Wesleyan University Press, 1967.

Beckett, Samuel. *Happy Days*. New York: Grove Press, 1959.

Bergmann, Gustav. "Intentionality." in *Intentionality, Mind and Language*. edited by Ausinio Marras. Chicago: The University of Illinois Press, 1972, 287-320.

Block, Ned. "Introduction: What is Innateness?" in *Readings in Philosophy of Psychology*, Volume 2, edited by Ned Block, Harvard University Press, 1981, 279-281.

Boff, Leonardo. "Trinitarian Community and Social Liberation," *Cross Currents*, Volume 38, #3, 1988, 289-308.

Brenner, Michael, editor. *The Structure of Action*. New York: St. Martin's Press, 1980.

Bruffee, Kenneth. *Collaborative Learning: Higher Education, Interdependence and the Authority of Knowledge*. Baltimore: The Johns Hopkins University Press, 1993.

Bruss, Elizabeth. *Autobiographical Acts: The Changing Situation of a Literary Genre*. Baltimore: The Johns Hopkins University Press, 1976.

Bultmann, Rudolf. *Jesus Christ and Mythology*. New York: Charles Scribner's Sons, 1958.

Burke, Kenneth. *A Rhetoric of Motives*. Los Angeles: The University of California Press, 1950.

——————. *A Grammar of Motives*. Los Angeles: The University of California Press, 1946.

Byron, William. "Catholic Education in a Pluralistic Society." *Origins*, March 15, 1990, Volume 19, #41, 669-675.

Capote, Truman. *In Cold Blood: A True Account of a Multiple Murder and Its Consequences*. A Signet Book: The New American Library, 1965.

Cavell, Stanley. "Politics as Opposed to What?" *Critical Theory*, September, 1982.

Chastain, Charles. "Reference and Context," in *Minnesota Studies in the Philosophy of Science*, Volume VII, *Language, Mind, and Knowledge*, edited by Keith Gunderson. Minneapolis: The University of Minnesota Press, 1975.

Chaucer, Geoffrey. *The Complete Prose and Poetry of Geoffrey Chaucer*. Edited by John H. Fisher. New York: Holt, Rinehart and Winston, 1977.

Chomsky, Noam, Hilary Putnam and Nelson Goodman. "Symposium on Innate Ideas." *The Philosophy of Language*. ed. John Searle. Oxford University Press, 1971.

——————. "Reply to Putnam," Chapter 16 in *Readings in Philosophy of Psychology*, Volume 2, edited by Ned Block, Harvard University Press, 1981, 301-304.

——————. "The 'Innateness Hypothesis' and Explanatory Models of Linguistics," Chapter 1 of *Readings in Philosophy of Psychology*, Volume 2, edited by Ned Block, Harvard University Press, 1981, 292-299.

-------. "Discussion of Putnam's Comments," Chapter Twenty in *Readings in Philosophy of Psychology*, Volume 1, edited by Ned Block, Harvard University Press, 1981, 349-358.

-------. "Topics in the Theory of Generative Grammar," in *Readings in Philosophy of Psychology*, Volume 2, edited by Ned Block, Harvard University Press,71-100.

-------. "Knowledge and Language." in *Minnesota Studies in the Philosophy of Science*, Volume VII, *Language, Mind, and Knowledge*, edited by Keith Gunderson. Minneapolis: The University of Minnesota Press, 1975.

-------. "Current Issues in Linguistic Theory," in *The Structure of Language: Readings in the Philosophy of Language*. edited by Jerry A. Fodor and Jerrold J. Katz. New Jersey: Prentice- Hall, Inc., 1964.

-------. "A Transformational Approach to Syntax." in *The Structure of Language: Readings in the Philosophy of Language*. edited by Jerry A. Fodor and Jerrold J. Katz. New Jersey: Prentice- Hall, Inc., 1964.

Clark, Herbert H. and Peter Lucy. "Understanding What is Meant from What is Said: A Study in Conversationally Conveyed Requests," *Journal of Verbal Learning and Verbal Behaviour* 14, 197, 56-72.

Cleminger, Bruce. "Griffioen Lectures Capacity Crowd," *Perspective: Institute for Christian Studies*, Volume 25, #1, February, 1991.

Cohen, L. Jonathan. "Do Illocutionary Forces Exist?" *Philosophical Quarterly*, XIV, No. 5 (1964), 118-137.

Church, Alonzo. "Propositions and Sentences." in *The Problem of Universals* (Notre Dame: University of Notre Dame Press, 1956), 3-11.

Culler, Jonathan. *Structuralist Poetics: Structuralism, Linguistics and the Study of Literature*. Ithaca, New York: Cornell University Press, 1975.

Davis, Mary Ann K. "DeQuincey's *Confessions*: A Strategy for Salvation," in *Christianity and Literature*, Volume XXXVIII. No. 3, Spring, 1989, 33-44.

Dennett, Daniel C. "Features of Intentional Action," *Philosophy and Phenomenological Research*, Volume 29, December, 1968, #2, 232-244.

-------. *Brainstorms: Philosophical Essays on Mind and Psychology*. Cambridge: MIT Press, 1961.

-------. "Brain Writing and Mind Reading." in *Minnesota Studies in the Philosophy of Science*, Volume VII, *Language, Mind, and Knowledge*, edited by Keith Gunderson. Minneapolis: The University of Minnesota Press, 1975.

DeQuincey, Thomas. *Selected Writings of Thomas DeQuincey*. Selected and edited with an Introduction by Philip Van Doren Stern, New York: The Modern Library, 1937.

————. *Confessions of an English Opium-Eater and Other Writings*. Edited with an introduction by Grevel Lindop. Oxford University Press, 1985.

Derrida, Jacques. *Of Grammatology*, trans. Gyatri Chakravorty Spivak. Baltimore: The Johns Hopkins University Press, 1974.

————. *The Ear of the Other: Otobiography, Transference, Translation*. Trans. Peggy Kamuf, ed. Christie McDonald. New York: Schocken Books, 1985.

————. *Margins of Philosophy*. The University of Chicago Press, 1972.

————. *Writing and Difference*. The University of Chicago Press, 1978.

Diamond, Cora and Jenny Teichman, editors. *Intention and Intentionality: Essays in Honour of G.E.M. Anscombe*. Ithaca: Cornell University Press, 1979.

Dretske, Fred. *Explaining Behaviour: Reasons in a World of Causes*. Cambridge, Mass.: MIT Press, 1988.

————. "Why Thinking Helps." Unpublished manuscript, 1988.

————. "Referring to Events." *Midwest Studies in Philosophy*, II, 1977, 90-99.

Devitt, Michael. "Why Fodor Can't Have It Both Ways." Unpublished manuscript, 1988.

Donnellan, Keith S. "Reference and Definite Descriptions." *Readings in the Philosophy of Language*, edited by Jay F. Rosenberg and Charles Travis, New Jersey: Prentice-Hall, Inc., 1971, 19-29.

Eckartsberg, Rolf von. "Maps of the Mind: The Cartography of Consciousness," in *The Metamorphosis of Consciousness*, New York: Plenum Press, 1981.

Edie, James M. *Speaking and Meaning: The Phenomenology of Language*. Indiana University Press, 1976.

Eliot, George. *Adam Bede*. London: Penguin Books, 1985.

Felman, Shoshana. *The Literary Speech Act: Don Juan with J.L. Austin, or Seduction in Two Languages*, translated by Catherine Porter. Ithaca: Cornell University Press, 1983.

Field, Hartry. "Mental Representation." in *Readings in Philosophy and Psychology*, Volume Two, edited by Ned Block, Harvard University Press, 1981, 78-114.

———. "Critical Notice: Robert Stalnaker, *Inquiry.*" *Philosophy of Science*, September, 1986, Volume 53, #3, 425-448.

———. "Stalnaker on Intentionality." *Pacific Philosophical Quarterly*, April, 1986, Volume 67, #2, 98-111.

———. "The Deflationary Conception of Truth," in *Fact, Science and Morality: Essays on A.J. Ayer's Language Truth and Logic*, edited by Graham Macdonald and Crispin Wright. London: Basil Blackwell Ltd., 1986, 55-117.

Fielding, Henry. *Joseph Andrews*. Edited by R.F. Brissenden. New York: Penguin Books, 1977.

Fodor, Jerry A. "Making Mind Matter More." Unpublished manuscript, September, 1988.

———. "Propositional Attitudes." in *Readings in Philosophy of Psychology*, Volume 2, edited by Ned Block. Harvard University Press, 1981, 45-63.

———. "Private Language, Public Languages," in *The Language of Thought*. New York: Thomas Y. Cromwell Company, 1975, 55-97.

Fowler, Roger. "The Referential Code and Narrative Authority." *Language and Style*, Volume 10, 1978.

Ghandi, Mohandas K. *Autobiography: The Story of My Experiments With Truth*, translated by Mahdev Desai. New York: Dover Publications, Inc.. 1983.

Gallagher, Joseph E. "Theology and Intention in Chaucer's *Troilus*," *Chaucer Review*, 7, 44-66.

Geach, Peter. "Assertions." *The Philosophical Review*, LXXIV, No.4 (1965), 449-465.

Goody, Jack. *The Domestication of the Savage Mind*. Cambridge University Press, 1977.

Gordon, Robert M. "Mental Simulation and the Explanation of Behaviour," Unpublished manuscript, October, 1988.

———. "Folk Psychology as Simulation." *Mind and Language*. Volume 1, No. 2 Summer, 1986. 158-171.

Greene, Graham. *The End of the Affair*. New York: Penguin Books, 1962.

———. *Monsignor Quixote*. New York: Penguin Books, 1982.

158

Grice, Paul. "Meaning Revisited." Chapter Five of *Mutual Knowledge*. Edited by Neil Smith. Corpus Christi, Texas: Academie Press, Inc., 1982.

--------. "Utterer's Meaning, Sentence-Meaning, and Word-Meaning," *Foundations of Language* (4) (1968), 1-18.

--------. *Intention and Uncertainty*. Annual Philosophical Lecture, Henriette Hertz Trust, British Academy,1971; from the Proceedings of the British Academy, Volume LVII, London: Oxford University Press.

Harris, Richard. "Memory and Comprehension of Implications and Inferences of Complex Sentences." *Journal of Verbal Learning and Verbal Behaviour*, 13, 1974, 626-637.

Harris, Zelig. "Discourse Analysis." in *The Structure of Language: Readings in the Philosophy of Language*. edited by Jerry A. Fodor and Jerrold J. Katz. New Jersey: Prentice-Hall, Inc., 1964.

Hemeren, Goram. "Intention and Interpretation in Literary Criticism." *New Literary History*. 7, 1, 1975, 57-82.

Holdcroft, David. *Words and Deeds: Problems in the Theory of Speech Acts*. Oxford: Clarendon Press, 1978.

Howard, Donald R. "Experience, Language and Consciousness: *Troilus and Criseyde*, II, 596-931," *Medieval Literature and Folklore Studies*, 173-192.

Hungerland, Isabel C. "Contextual Implication." *Inquiry*, 211-258.

Husserl, Edmund. *Ideas: General Introduction to Pure Phenomenology*. New York: Collier Books: a Division of Macmillan Publishing Co., Inc., 1931.

Ionesco, Eugene. *Four Plays: The Bald Soprano, The Lesson, Jack, or The Submission, The Chairs*, Translated by Donald M. Allen. New York: Grove Press, Inc., 1958.

Iser, Wolfgang, *The Act of Reading: A Theory of Aesthetic Response*. Baltimore: The Johns Hopkins University Press, 1978.

Jaynes, Julian. *The Origin of Consciousness in the Breakdown of the Bicameral Mind*. Houghton-Mifflin Company, 1976.

Katz, Jerrold J. "Innate Ideas," Chapter 14 in *Readings in Philosophy of Psychology*, Volume 2, edited by Ned Block, Harvard University Press, 1981, 282-291.

--------. "Logic and Language: An Examination of Recent Criticisms of Intensionalism," in *Minnesota Studies in the Philosophy of Science*, Volume VII, *Language, Mind, and Knowledge*, edited by Keith Gunderson. Minneapolis: The University of Minnesota Press, 1975.

Katz, Jerrold J. and Jerry A. Fodor. "The Structure of a Semantic Theory." in *The Structure of Language: Readings in the Philosophy of Language.* edited by Jerry A. Fodor and Jerrold J. Katz. New Jersey: Prentice-Hall, Inc., 1964.

———, editor. *The Philosophy of Linguistics.* Oxford University Press, 1985.

Kim, Jaegwon. "Causation, Emphasis, and Events." (Discussion of Dretske, "Referring to Events.") *Midwest Studies in Philosophy,* II, 1977, 100-103.

Lenneberg, Eric H. "The Capacity for Language Acquisition." in *The Structure of Language: Readings in the Philosophy of Language,* edited by Jerry A. Fodor and Jerrold J. Katz. New Jersey: Prentice-Hall, Inc., 1964.

Lemmon, E.J. "Sentences, Statements, and Propositions." in *Readings in the Philosophy of Language,* edited by Jay F. Rosenberg and Charles Travis. New Jersey: Prentice-Hall, Inc., 1971, 233-249.

LePore, Ernest and Barry Loewer. "Mind Matters." *The Journal of Philosophy,* 1987, 630-642.

Levi-Strauss, Claude. *The Raw and the Cooked: Introduction to a Science of Mythology.* New York: Harper & Row, 1969.

Lewis, C. S. *The Abolition of Man, or Reflections on Education with Special Reference to the Teaching of English in the Upper Forms of School.* New York: The Macmillan Co., 1947.

Lonergan, Bernard. *Doctrinal Pluralism.* The 1971 Pere Marquette Theology Lecture, Milwaukee: Marquette University Press, 1971.

Mayoux, Jean-Jacques. "Variations on the Time-Sense in *Tristram Shandy,*" in *Laurence Sterne's Tristram Shandy: An Authoritative Text, the Author of the Novel, Criticism.* Edited by Howard Anderson. New York: W.W. Norton and Company, 1980.

Merton, Thomas. "Marxism and Monastic Perspectives." Appendix VII of *The Asian Journal of Thomas Merton.* New York: New Directions Publishing Corporation, 1973, 326-343.

———. *The Sign of Jonas.* New York: Harcourt, Brace and Company, 1953.

Min, Anselm. "The Challenge of Radical Pluralism." *Cross Currents,* Volume 38, #3, 1988, 268-275.

Mizener, Arthur. "Character and Action in the Case of Criseyde," *PMLA,* LIV, 1939, 6-81.

Mott, Michael. *The Seven Mountains of Thomas Merton.* Boston: Houghton Mifflin Company, 1984.

160

Nabokov, Vladimir. *Speak, Memory: An Autobiography Revisited.* New York: G.P. Putnam's Sons, 1947, 1948, 1949, 1950, 1960, 1966.

The New Jerusalem Bible. Garden City: New York: Doubleday and Company, Inc., 1985.

Newman, John Henry. *An Essay on the Development of Christian Doctrine.* University of Notre Dame Press, 1989.

O'Connor, Flannery. *The Violent Bear It Away,* in *Flannery O'Connor Collected Works* published in New York: The Library of America, 1988, 329-480.

Olson, David. "What is Said and What is Meant in Speech and Writing." *Visible Language.* XVI, 2,1982, 115-174.

Ong, Walter. "Realizing Catholicism: Faith, Learning and the Future," *Theology Digest* 37: 4 Winter, 1990, 333-340.

Osberg, Richard H. "Between the Motion and the Act: Intentions and Ends in Chaucer's *Troilus.*" *Journal of English Literary History*, Summer, 1981, 48, 2, 257-270.

Pannikar, Raimundo. "Chosenness and Universality: Can Christians Claim Both?" *Cross Currents*, Volume 38, #3, 1988, 309-324.

Pinker, Steven. *The Language Instinct.* New York: William Morrow and Company, Inc., 1994.

Pitcher, George. "Propositions and the Correspondence Theory of Truth." in *Readings in the Philosophy of Language.* Edited by Jay F. Rosenberg and Charles Travis. New Jersey: Prentice- Hall, Inc., 1971, 223-233.

Plato: The Collected Dialogues. Edited by Edith Hamilton and Huntington Cairn. Princeton University Press: Bollingen Series LXXI, 1961.

Putnam, Hilary. "What is Innate and Why." in *Readings in Philosophy of Psychology*, Volume 2, edited by Ned Block, Harvard University Press, 1981, 339- 348.

--------. "Comment on Chomsky's Reply," Chapter 21 in *Readings in Philosophy of Psychology*, Volume 2, edited by Ned Block, Harvard University Press, 1981, 359-360.

--------. "The Meaning of 'Meaning,'" in *Minnesota Studies in the Philosophy of Science*, Volume VII, *Language, Mind, and Knowledge*, edited by Keith Gunderson. Minneapolis: The University of Minnesota Press, 1975.

Quillen, Keith. "Propositional Attitudes and Psychological Explanation." *Mind and Language.* Vol.1, No. 2, Summer, 1986, 133-157.

Restak, Richard M. *The Mind*. New York: Bantam Books, 1988.

Roberts, James. "Priest's Plea to the Pope: Hear Us," *The Province*, September 16, 1984, p. 29.

Sadock, Jerrold M. *Toward a Linguistic Theory of Speech Acts*. New York: Academic Press, 1974.

Sagan, Carl. *The Dragons of Eden: Speculations on the Evolution of Human Intelligence*. New York: Random House, 1977.

Schaubner, Ellen and Ellen Spolsky. "Conversational Noncooperation: The Case of Chaucer's Pardoner," *Language and Style*, 16 (1983), 249-261.

Schiffer, Stephen. "Intentionality and the Language of Thought," Chapter Four of *Remnants of Meaning*. Cambridge, Mass.: MIT Press, 1987, 73-110.

-------. "Stalnaker's Problem of Intentionality." *Pacific Philosophical Quarterly*, 67 (1986), 87-97.

-------. "Truth and the Theory of Content." in *Meaning and Understanding*, edited by Herman Parret and Jacques Bouveresse. New York: Walter de Gruyter Press, 1981, 204-222.

-------. "Naming and Knowing." *Midwest Studies in Philosophy*, II, 1977, 28-41.

Searle, John. "Proper Names." *Mind*. LXVII, no. 266 (1958), 166- 173.

-------. *Intentionality: An Essay in the Philosophy of Mind*. Cambridge University Press, 1983.

-------. *Foundations of Illocutionary Logic*. Cambridge University Press, 1985.

-------. *Expression and Meaning: Studies in the Theory of Speech Acts*. Cambridge University Press, 1979.

Smith, Frank. *Understanding Reading: A Psycholinguistic Analysis of Reading and Learning to Read*. New York: Holt, Rinehart and Winston, 1971.

-------. *Writing and the Writer*. New York: Holt, Rinehart and Winston, 1982.

Spivak, Gayatri Chakravorty, "Translator's Introduction," to *Of Grammatology*. Baltimore: The Johns Hopkins University Press, 1974.

Stalnaker, Robert C. *Inquiry*. Cambridge, Mass.: MIT Press, 1984.

-------. "Replies to Schiffer and Field." *Pacific Philosophical Quarterly*, 67 (1986), 113-123.

Stich, Stephen. *From Folk Psychology to Cognitive Science: The Case Against Belief*. Cambridge, Mass.: MIT Press, 1983.

Stokes, Myra. "Wordes White: Disingenuity in *Troilus and Criseyde.*" *English Studies*, February, 1983, 64 (1), 18-29.

Taylor, Karla. "A Text and its Afterlife: Dante and Chaucer." *Comparative Literature*, Winter, 1983 (3)(1) 1-20.

Taylor, Ann M. "Criseyde's 'Thought' in *Troilus and Criseyde* (II, 598-812)," *American Notes and Queries* 17: 18-19.

Thiemann, Ronald F. "In Praise of Pluralism," *The Thomist*. Volume 53, 1989, 489-503.

Van, Thomas A. "Criseyde's Indirections," *American Notes and Queries* 13 (1974) 34-365.

Vance, Eugene. "'Mervelous Signals': Poetics, Sign Theory, and Politics in Chaucer's *Troilus*," *New Literary History* X (1979), 293-335.

Vanderveken, Daniel. "Some Philosophical Remarks on the Theory of Types in Intensional Logic." *Erkenntnis*, 17, (1982) 85-112.

von Balthasar, Hans Urs. *Truth is Symphonic: Aspects of Christian Pluralism.* trans. by Graham Harrison. San Francisco, Ignatius Press, 1987.

Watson, Lawrence. "Understanding a Life History as a Subjective Document: Hermeneutical and Phenomenological Perspectives." *Ethos*, 1976, Volume 4.

Williams, Tennessee. *The Glass Menagerie*. New York: A Signet Book of the New American Library, 1945.

Wimsatt, W.K. and Monroe C. Beardsley. "The Intentional Fallacy," and "The Affective Fallacy," in Hazard Adams' *Critical Theory Since Plato*, New York: Harcourt Brace Jovanovich, Inc., 1971, pp. 1014 ff.

Index